May you
and ble

MW01178839

7th June 2021

FRANKLY SPEAKING

120 Matter-of-Fact and
Thought Provoking Readings

Janet Dash-Harris

CLM PUBLISHING

FRANKLY SPEAKING
120 Matter-of-Fact and Thought Provoking Readings

ISBN: 978-0-9965501-1-6

Contact the author JANET DASH-HARRIS
ELPJH@YAHOO.COM

Published by CLM Publishing
www.shop.clmpublishing.com
Grand Cayman, Cayman Islands

Printed in the United States of America

DEDICATION

To the memory of my dearly departed parents, Elton (Cephas) and Gwendoline Dash.

To my husband Lincoln, whose unconditional love and support has made this a reality.

To my son Jamal and granddaughter Kassidee, whom I cherish dearly.

And to God - who has made everything possible.

Be Blessed,

Janet Dash-Harris

CONTENTS

"He who began a good work in you will carry it on to completion until the day of Christ Jesus" (Philippians 1:6).

"In the last days, God says, I will pour out my Spirit on all people. Your sons and daughters will prophesy, your young men will see visions, your old men will dream dreams" (Acts 2:17).

ACKNOWLEDGEMENTS

First and foremost, I want to thank Almighty God for the wisdom and knowledge bestowed upon me in writing this book, for the strength He gave to me to persevere and complete it, for His unfailing favour and blessing each step of the way and His unwavering faithfulness.

I am indeed indebted to my dear husband, Lincoln, for his continued support, advice and encouragement.

Thanks also to Elsa Bobb, wife of my Pastor Torrance Bobb, who rekindled my desire to write a book.

Special thanks to my very dear friends, Kim Williams, Sandra Yarde, Deborah Lynch-Theobalds, Dr. Earl Robinson and Andrea Lashley for their insight, words of wisdom and constructive criticism. It would be remiss of me if I did not thank CLM Publisher Karen Chin who truly went beyond the call of duty in getting this book ready for publication.

And to all my other friends on my special Word of the Day broadcast list, I thank you immensely.

INTRODUCTION

I have always had a passion for reading and it is that insatiable desire that sparked my interest in writing.

My initiation was in the 1980s when I started composing poems for the National Independence Festival of Creative Arts (NIFCA) in Barbados. I developed a special love for acrostic writing and penned several to honour persons on special occasions.

In 2009 while recuperating after major surgery, I started compiling a book of short poems, but never completed it. Again in 2014 after attending a presentation by my Pastor's wife and being encouraged to actively take up writing, I started piecing together an autobiography, but once again the manuscript was shelved.

Finally, after my mother died in March 2015, in an effort to encourage myself, I started sharing a verse a day to my WhatsApp friends. Around the same time my best friend Kim Williams issued me a Facebook challenge to share a verse for seven consecutive days. I found myself eagerly looking forward to doing so. Those verses eventually blossomed into full-fledged daily devotionals, some of which are autobiographical in nature, which I have now put together. I trust they will be a blessing to your heart.

The WOW Factor

Do you know that there is an answer for EVERYTHING we face?

Relationship issues, conflict, money worries, sickness, persecution, hurt, unforgiveness, being misunderstood, being wronged, false accusations and the list can go on. The TRUE answer is not found in the advice of friends or family or inspirational readings, (though you may find some guidance) and certainly not in daily horoscope predictions. Your answer IS in the word of God, the BIBLE, which is powerful and *sharper than any two-edged sword, piercing even to the division of soul and spirit, and of joints and marrow, and is a discerner of the thoughts and intents of the heart"* Hebrews 4:12.

Not sure how you should deal with a matter? Search the scriptures. You'll find your answer there.

It's the WOW factor! The Wonder Of the Word. Enjoy your reading.

1

Whose Report?

At some point in every student's career he or she will be given a report on their progress (or lack thereof). For the pupils who have worked hard, been conscientious and lived up to their potential there is very little to dread, but for those who do not maximize the opportunities afforded them at school, there is often a reluctance to show their parents their report. Some may even try to doctor it a bit. I heard a story once of a student who tried to con her mother into believing that the C's, D's and E's on her report were actual signs of progress. She told her mum that C meant "Coming along," D was a "Distinction" and "E" was Excellent. The mother was very pleased to say the least. However, that report couldn't have been further from the truth.

It was when her mum finally came to the school that the record was set straight and she was told exactly how her daughter was doing and realizing that she had been duped distressed this lady very much.

On August 18, 2004, the occasion of our 3rd anniversary, my husband and I sat in a consultant gynaecologist's office in England only to hear him pronounce the dreaded words,

"You have ovarian cancer and we have scheduled you for surgery. You will also need to undergo chemo treatment." What news ... and on our anniversary too!

I had recently suffered a miscarriage. The doctor explained that his diagnosis was as a result of an extremely elevated CA125 reading in the thousands! That didn't mean much to me, until the doctor said that it should be between 1 and 14, in response to my question about what it should be. To say we were devastated is to put it mildly. Suddenly the joys of a holiday were meaningless. We were both in tears. An oncology nurse was on stand by and she led us away to discuss our "options." They seemed to have thought of everything. Except one thing! My God's ability to turn around a seemingly impossible situation.

When we left that hospital my first reaction was to call my Pastors in Barbados and the Cayman Islands to inform them and to ask the church to be in prayer on my behalf. They agreed and I too went into 3 days of prayer and fasting. On my return to the doctor three days later, the CA125 level had subsided tremendously. While it was not down to the required level I was still overjoyed. There had been a break through. Psalm 18:6 was real, *"In my distress I called to the LORD; I cried to my God for help. From his temple He heard my voice; my cry came before Him, into His ears."*

The operation went ahead as planned on September 5, and my right ovary which contained a cyst was removed. I stayed in the hospital for less than a week. Thinking that I had been told by the doctor that my CA125 level had now reached 7, the nurse unwittingly shared that information with me, then swore me to secrecy when she realized I was ignorant of the fact. Unable to explain what had taken place here is what the doctor wrote in his report: *"As you are aware, the histology did not show any evidence of malignancy and the whole pattern of CA125 levels is an interesting one which I have not seen before."* When he read it to me I told him it was God who had done it. Romans 4:17 tells us, *"He is our father in the sight of God, in whom he believed--the God who gives life to the dead and calls into being things that were not."* James 5:15 is not simply make believe. It tells us clearly, *"And the prayer offered in faith will make the sick person well; the Lord will raise them up."*

God is our Jehovah Rophe, our healer, a fact emphasized in Isaiah 53:5, *"But he was pierced for our transgressions, He was crushed for our iniquities; the punishment that brought us peace was on Him, and by His wounds we are healed."*

This was clearly a lesson in declaring and believing the word of God over what the doctor had decreed. It just goes to show that even when the situation seems to be at its bleakest we should choose to believe the report of the Lord and we will not be disappointed.

2

Tough But Good!

My husband, Lincoln is one of the most incredible men you will ever meet. Although we share some things in common in other ways we are so uniquely different. I guess that's why they say unlike poles attract; like poles repel. I am very talkative while he is more the silent type. I thoroughly enjoy shopping. He, not so much. He loves to cook. I like to eat. Though we both own a few matching pairs of sketchers, another distinct difference is our shoe size. I have big flat feet - US size 11 to be precise - while his are small and neat (Size 8). It is very true to say I could never fill his shoes. Well, I could - but I'd have some foot left over. The most outstanding difference though is in our attitude. I often say that if I was half as nice as he is we would be a perfect couple. I have to admit though that sometimes I think he's just a bit too nice especially when I think others are taking advantage of him. But as a Christian, is it possible to be too nice? If ever you ask him how he is doing, his standard answer is always, "I'm good. " He is never one to lament and he doesn't complain. He is the first to volunteer his services and he gives without even considering how and if he might be repaid. All of this despite losing his job and not because of being a poor performer.

Quite the contrary! After three-and-a-half years in which he was a star performer who only stayed away from work for half of a day (his boss sent him home because he was visibly sick), he was informed that they would be forced to let him go because of an immigration ruling. Some people in a similar position might have slackened off, but not Lincoln. He continued to give of his very best and still maintains cordial relations with all of the staff there to this day. As if that wasn't enough in 2012 he was diagnosed with prostate cancer.

Following an 8 hour operation to remove the prostate and 39 difficult days of radiation treatment, I can't help but salute his resolve not to let anything get him down. Only recently when I was complaining about something he lovingly rebuked me, by telling me that he was becoming the Christian that I always used to encourage (not nag) him to become and that I should be glad. I thought for a moment and considered that when you are daily facing a life threatening illness like he and many others are, all the other challenges of life pale in comparison.

The following passages come to mind when I consider him:

> *"Though he slay me, yet will I hope in him; I will surely defend my ways to his face."* Job 13:15

> *"Do not merely listen to the word, and so deceive yourselves. Do what it says."* James 1:22

> *"In your relationships with one another, have the same mindset as Christ Jesus."* Philippians 2:5

> *"Do not conform to the pattern of this world, but be transformed by the renewing of your mind. Then you will be able to test and approve what God's will is--His good, pleasing and perfect will."* Romans 12:2

> *"I know what it is to be in need, and I know what it is to have plenty. I have learned the secret of being content in any and every situation, whether well fed or hungry, whether living in plenty or in want."* Philippians 4:12

> *"I consider that our present sufferings are not worth comparing with the glory that will be revealed in us."* Romans 8:18

Life sure may be tough at times but God is still good!

3

Janet Harris C.G.

C.G.? Now what on earth is that?

I always marvel when I receive emails these days, as there is a growing trend in which many persons are affixing a bunch of letters after their name - B.A., B. Sc., M.A., M.Sc., A.Sc., Ph.D., A.C.C.A., C.P.A., C.G.A. M. Phil. - as part of their signature. Truth be told, although I know they are educational qualifications of some sort, (and I too have a couple), I don't even know what some of them mean, but what is clear to me is that they are of great importance to them.

I am not suggesting for a minute that enhancing your qualifications while improving your education is not to be commended, but when Jesus returns that won't matter one iota. I remember listening to the obituary of a man being read on the radio. Boy, did the list of qualifications and positions held in his lifetime seem impressive!

Spontaneously, I said aloud, "Still dead." I only realized my mum had been listening when she laughed and I later overheard her repeating the incident to friends. You may argue that Jesus tells us in Luke 19:13 to, "*Occupy until He comes*," which suggests we should make the most of our time on earth, but what He expects of us in occupying is to take charge of the Church that He established and maintain it in righteousness. In so doing we would be obeying the command in Matthew 5:16 to, "*Let your light so shine before men, that they may see your good works, and glorify your Father which is in heaven.*" Ephesians 5:27 makes it clear that Jesus is returning for, "*A radiant church, without stain or wrinkle or any other blemish, but holy and blameless.*" When He returns to judge the world, His main focus will be: Was His offer accepted or rejected? And consequently, "Is your name written in the Lamb's Book of Life?"

At that time having a B.A., B. Sc., M.A., M.Sc., A.Sc., Ph.D., A.C.C.A., C.P.A., C.G.A. or M. Phil. won't matter at all. The most important designation will be C. G., CHILD of GOD, the only qualification that will stand you in good stead. Mark 8:36 (KJV) asks the question of us all, *"For what shall it profit a man, if he shall gain the whole world, and lose his own soul?"*

Thinking about enhancing your qualifications? Then put C.G. top of your list.

4

The ABC of God

Who is God to you?

Janet Jackson once recorded a song entitled, "What have you done for me lately?"[1] During the intro to the song there is a dialogue between the singer and one of her girlfriends, in which Janet is lamenting that she has been disappointed yet again by the boyfriend with whom she is so madly in love. She recalls the deeds he had done for her in the past but she is now forced to accept that things have changed and he has done nothing recently for her, prompting her to ask the question of him, "What have you done for me lately?"

Our God is not a God of disappointments or failure. Whatever He says, He does.

According to Isaiah 55:10-11,

> "As the rain and the snow come down from heaven, and do not return to it without watering the earth and making it bud and flourish, so that it yields seed for the sower and bread for the eater, so is my word that goes out from my mouth: It will not return to me empty, but will accomplish what I desire and achieve the purpose for which I sent it."

Mull over the events of the past year and you ask of God, "What have you done for me lately?"

You will discover that He was, is and will continue to be...

---

[1] Janet Jackson, Control, 1986

Alive/Awesome/All that/Alpha
Brilliant
Conqueror/Controller
Divine/Deliverer
Everything/Excellent/Eternal/Effective
Faithful/Forever/Forgiving
Great/God/Guide
Holy/High and lifted up/Healer
Indescribable/Impenetrable/Immutable
Just/Jealous/Jehovah Jireh
King of Kings
Lord of Lords/Leader/Lion of Judah
Majestic/Miracle worker
Noteworthy/Nurturing
Omnipotent/Omniscient/Omega
Patient/Pure/Passionate/Protector
Quality extraordinaire
Real/Righteous/Rock/Revealer
Saviour/Strength/Shield
Triumphant
Uncontainable/Unique
Victorious
Wise/Winner
Xtraordinary
Yahweh
Zealous

What a mighty God! Who is He to you? Remind yourself.

5

Bride or Bridesmaid?

Proverbs 15:33 states, *"Wisdom's instruction is to fear the Lord, and humility comes before honour."* Often times we feel like we are always in the bridesmaid's position and we wonder, "Will I ever be the bride? Will I ever get that home or that car or that healing or that job or the promotion or the answer to the prayers I have prayed over and over?"

The word today is a reminder that before we can be elevated we need to humble ourselves. Be contented with what you have now. This doesn't mean that better is not in store for you. It means we need to wait and wait patiently before receiving what God has promised.

Remember God CANNOT lie. He tells us in Jeremiah 29:11 that He *"knows the plans He has for us, plans to prosper us and not to harm us, to give us hope and a future."* And that is a bright future, but sometimes we need to be taken down from our high horses to that place where we are totally surrendered to God, recognizing that ALL power is in His hands. So while we wait for Him to reveal His awesome power in our lives, let us try to not hasten the process but let's stay in our "small" corner and be patient, praising and thanking Him in the meantime, knowing that greater is coming!

Proverbs 16:3-4 tells us, *"Commit to the Lord whatever you do, and He will establish your plans. The Lord works out everything to its proper end."* Don't be too quick to make decisions especially those that can have long lasting and life changing results. Take everything to God in prayer FIRST. Often times we listen to the advice of friends and family - not that this is always a bad thing - but we need to get to the place where God is the one we consult first. For sure He won't give us bad advice or be forced to change His mind for His ways are sure. To find out what He Is saying to us we need to dedicate ourselves to studying His word for it is a *"lamp unto our feet and a light unto our path"* Psalm 119:105.

The songwriter reminds us:

Oh what peace we often forfeit
Oh what needless pains we bear
All because we do not carry everything to God in prayer[2].

Reduce your regrets. Be guided by God.

---

[2] Joseph M Scriven, *What a Friend We Have in Jesus.*

6

Seize the POP!

In John 14: 12-14 Jesus states,

> *"He who believes in Me, the works that I do he will do also; and greater works than these he will do, because I go to My Father. And whatever you ask in My name, that I will do, that the Father may be glorified in the Son. If you ask anything in My name, I will do it"*

Jesus has told us what our capabilities are. Don't underestimate what you can accomplish and what strongholds you can tear down when you pray in the name of Jesus.

"God's word is our spiritual weapon against the realm of darkness and when we align our will with God's will, we will see the enemy pushed back" (Stormie Omartian).[3]

When we lose things that are important to us - loved ones, relationships, jobs, finances, health etc. etc. - or our world seems to be caving in on us, remember God is still on the throne and though we may be devastated He is not. He still sees the great plan and purpose for our life even if we can't at that time. The enemy wants to steal that bright future from us but through constant warring in prayer we can fight for and achieve what God has destined for us.

Remember *"the prayer of a righteous man is powerful and effective"* (James 5:16). So, seize the POP, - the Power Of Prayer.

---

[3] Stormie Omartian, *Prayer Warrior, 2013*

7

The FIG Route

Life is like a drive and it's all about routes. The question is what route will you take?

The word for you today is: Choose the FIG route. There is an adage that says seeing is believing. However, Hebrews 11:1 tells us, *Now faith is confidence in what we hope for and assurance about what we do not see."* What are you believing and trusting God for? Does it seem impossible? Unlikely? Don't focus on what you are seeing with your natural eye. Focus on what His word says. Psalm 84:11 states, *"No good thing does He withhold from those whose walk is blameless."*

The night before Paul and his crew were shipwrecked an angel of the Lord appeared to him and assured him that not one of their lives would be lost and he was able to declare to the crew in Acts 27:25: *"So keep up your courage, men, for I have faith in God that it will happen just as he told me."* And you know what? It did.

According to Isaiah 55:11, *"so is my word that goes out from my mouth: It will not return to me empty, but will accomplish what I desire and achieve the purpose for which I sent it."* So as a child of God don't be thrown off course by the challenges of this world. Just choose the FIG route - Faith In God route.

8

Don't Forget to TOP Up!

As cell phone users, it's impossible to use our phones if they are turned off. It's also important to ensure that we have credit, whether prepaid or post-paid, to send that message or to make that call. Even if we opt to only use WIFI to cut down on data charges, we need to find a "hot spot" to do so. To do this we have to have an available network. Some WIFI networks though are secured and we need a password to gain access.

God is our secure network, but He has made the password available to us. That password is Jesus - the source of all power and authority. In John 16:23-24 Jesus says, *"Whatever you ask the Father in my name He will give you. Until now you have asked nothing in my name. Ask, and you will receive, that your joy may be full."*

Don't think that we are just mere mortals, for in response to the question,

> *"What is man that you are mindful of him, or the son of man that you take care of him?" the response is, "You have made him a little lower than the angels; you have crowned him with glory and honour, and set him over the works of Your hands. You have put all things in subjection under his feet" (Hebrews 2: 6-8).*

Never underestimate what you can do when you connect to God and pray in the name of Jesus. Regardless to your circumstance though, you need to TOP up first - Turn On the Power - and stay connected to the source - Jesus - for "There is power in the name of Jesus to break EVERY chain." Have a powerful day!

9

Stay At The Crease!

Life is like a game of cricket. The batting team tries to score as many runs as possible, while the job of the fielding side is to make sure that doesn't happen. The bowlers on the fielding side are the main strike force. Their aim? To get the batsman out and to do so quickly and they have a range of tactics. They'll bowl the ball at a ferocious speed, or slow it down significantly. They'll spin the ball or keep it low. You may get a bouncer or a yorker or a googly or you may be adjudged trapped LBW (Leg Before Wicket). You may hit the ball and be out caught by a fielder or they just might clean bowl you. Occasionally though the bowler may step over his line and the umpire who is in charge of the game will shout, "No ball!"

This means that regardless to the outcome of that ball bowled by the bowler you cannot be out, except of course you decide to make a run for it and you are "run out". Our enemy, the devil, is the captain of the fielding side and we are on the batting side. His aim is to get us out and he will try every trick he can think of. Don't forget he is described in 1 Peter 5: 8 as prowling around *like a roaring lion looking for someone he may devour,"* and in John 10:10 as a thief who comes to, *"steal, kill and destroy."* Jesus is our captain and He is a master tactician.

He is not LIKE a lion. He IS THE CONQUERING LION! And He has come that, *"We may have life and have it in abundance."* John 10:10. God is the umpire, the one in charge of the game. Our job as the batting side is to stay at the crease and bat as long as we can to ensure that victory is ours. When the devil bowls the no balls in your life stay in the crease. Don't try to make a run for it and risk being run out. Our aim is to be able to say, like the apostle Paul in 2 Timothy 4 : 7, *"I have fought a good fight, I have finished my course, I have kept the faith,*" so that we can hear the reply, "*Well done, good and faithful servant; enter into the joy of the Lord*" (Matthew 25:23) so that we can receive the "*crown of righteousness which the Lord, the righteous judge shall give to us*" (2 Timothy 4: 8). We are assured of victory. Just remember to stay in your crease and bat!

10

Follow Each DOT

Have you ever done a join the dot activity before? It's like a map. You follow dot after dot after dot and at the end a picture of some sort is revealed. You don't always get a prize for doing it, but you do feel this sense of accomplishment. Sometimes, however, you may make a mistake and if you don't follow the path correctly the final image may seem recognizable, but it is not what it should be. It's distorted. The Christian walk is one of following the DOT, God's road map for successful living. The Bible is that map and because God knows the importance of following His DOT He gives us constant reminders to help us ensure that we will get the real picture. Joshua 1: 8 states, *"Keep this Book of the Law always on your lips; meditate on it day and night, so that you may be careful to do everything written in it. Then you will be prosperous and successful."*

Another DOT is in Proverbs 3:1-2 *"My son, do not forget my teaching, but keep my commands in your heart, for they will prolong your life many years and bring you peace and prosperity."*

Still another guiding DOT in 2 Peter 1:3-4 states,

> *"His divine power has given us everything we need for a godly life through our knowledge of him who called us by his own glory and goodness. Through these he has given us His very great and precious promises, so that through them you may participate in the divine nature, having escaped the corruption in the world caused by evil desires."*

When we read God's word and we follow correctly each DOT that He has laid out for us, not only will we get a sense of satisfaction for having formed the correct image but there will also be the added reward.

> [10]*"Therefore, my brothers and sisters, make every effort to confirm your calling and election. For if you do these things you will never stumble, [11]and you will receive a rich welcome into the eternal kingdom of our Lord and Saviour Jesus Christ."* 2 Peter 1:10-11

However, we have to be careful not to compromise the word, because it will cause us to deviate from the path and the result would be a distorted picture. So follow each DOT - Divine Ordained Truth - so that the true picture can be revealed and you can claim the prize that has been promised.

11

Just SIT

Psalm 66:1-2 tells us to, "*Make a joyful noise unto God, all ye lands: Sing forth the honour of his name: make His praise glorious.*" But if we are really honest very few things can compare to listening to someone singing a song who repeatedly goes off key or sings out of tune or a CD that is scratched. The sound just makes you flinch.

No matter how great a singer or a choir is, if they are not in tune it takes away from the beauty of the song. That's why they'll spend hours on end practising and practising until they've got it right. They need to listen to the music over and over and be guided by the choir director whom they trust to help them get it right. I've never known a musical director to mislead those for whom he/she has responsibility. After all when the singers deliver a flawless rendition the director gets kudos too!

Let's think of God as our Choir Director. We need to get to know His voice, listen to His directions and follow His lead. John 10:27 tells us "*My sheep listen to my voice; I know them, and they follow me.*" When we obey God's word and "*Let our light shine before others, they will see our good works and glorify our father in heaven.*" Matthew 5:16. So don't go off key. Just SIT - Stay In Tune.

12

He's the PITS

June 1 to November 30 is designated as hurricane season in the Caribbean and many people just dread hearing that "H" word. For some it conjures up all kinds of awful images. If you've ever experienced one before the fear is even greater. As a matter of fact the knowledge of an impending storm causes such anxious moments that for many the adrenaline levels just seem to keep on rising.

The threat of any storm is often accompanied by warnings and repeated advisories stating that if you want to minimize the potential risks you would do well to be prepared. Sometimes as an added measure schools and businesses are forced to close and some people even leave their homes and go to a shelter. Though the best precautions won't avert the storm, eventually, after all the preparations have been made, the storm will pass by, sometimes almost unnoticed, and you breathe a sigh of relief.

There are others however, who forget about the adage "Better to be safe than sorry, "as they grumble about the "inconvenience they have suffered." Sometimes though after a while of constant preparation followed by no storms, it is possible that complacency may step in and you may go easy on the preparations until you may decide not to make any at all. And then the big one comes and you are UNPREPARED. Life in general is characterized by storms, but God offers us shelter and His peace. We are told in Psalm 46:1 that, "*God is our refuge and strength; a very present help in the time of trouble.*"

Once Jesus and his disciples were crossing a lake and a terrible storm arose. Jesus, though, was sleeping at the time. The disciples were naturally scared and they woke him and said, "*Teacher, don't you care if we drown?*" Jesus' immediate reaction was to rebuke the wind and speak to the waves and say, *"Peace! Be still!"* and immediately the wind died down and it was completely calm (Mark 4:35-39). Jesus still offers that peace today.

In John 14:27 He says, *"Peace I leave with you; my Peace I give you. I do not give to you as the world gives. Do not let your hearts be troubled and do not be afraid."* So when those dreadful storms of life arise, as they will surely do, don't be caught off guard.

Though you may feel afraid, remember to turn to Jesus. He really is the PITS - Peace In The Storm. Have a peaceful day.

13

Give Me The Gem!

They say that diamonds are a girl's best friend. Maybe it's because they are pretty and expensive! Their cost, for sure, renders them very valuable and the gift of diamonds or any other precious stone or exquisite piece of jewelry is sure to bring a smile to a loved one's face. After receiving them some persons even go as far as insuring them and/or choosing to wear them only on special occasions. But do you know that no matter how expensive these items of jewelry are, they will not last forever?

Matthew 6:19-21 cautions us,

> *"Do not store up for yourselves treasures on earth where moth and rust destroy and where thieves break in and steal. But store up for yourselves treasures in heaven, where moth and vermin do not destroy, and where thieves do not break in and steal. For where your treasure is, there your heart will be also."*

Although many people relish receiving precious stones as a gift, some may never be that fortunate to receive such in their lifetime.

But God offers us all a GEM of another kind - one that money can't buy yet is valuable, effective and long-lasting. He gives us His Grace, His unmerited favour and His power. When Zerubbabel was given the task of rebuilding the temple, he faced challenges which seemed insurmountable and he doubted whether he would accomplish the awesome task which lay before him.

However, God assured him it would happen, *"Not by might nor by power, but by my Spirit,"* (Zechariah 4:6). Zerubbabel was then instructed by God to speak grace to the mountain, *"Who are you, O great mountain? Before Zerubbabel you shall become a plain! And he shall bring forth the capstone with shouts of 'Grace, grace to it!'* (Zechariah 4:7).

When we face the mountains in our life, those challenges that seem insurmountable, speak God's enabling grace to them and watch them disintegrate and become plains. We are reminded in 2 Corinthians 12: 9 that God's *"grace is sufficient for [us], for [His] power is made perfect in [our] weakness."* So take God's GEM - Grace Exterminating Mountains. Have a gracious day!

14

I Confess

This word is more of a confession and it is LONG!

They say that confession is good for the soul. If I had any doubt that these words I have been sharing with you were God ordained, I am absolutely sure after this personal experience that they most definitely are and that is why I must share it with you. When I wake in the morning I ask God to tell me what to write and He does, there and then. So the word is NOT decided by me.

One morning shortly after starting these broadcast messages, my husband Lincoln woke me up with these words, "Don't you have to send out the word of the day?" It was about 6:15, which for me was late. Anyway I started and the word was "Put on the LOG." I worked and worked on it, but at 7:15 I still wasn't finished. Instead of driving to school as I normally do I asked him to drive instead so that I could continue working on this word. At 9:20 I was almost finished and was proof reading it, when I paused to make a call to Lincoln. He was still at the school, waiting for me to complete a task for him which I had promised to do for a while.

Imagine my horror and utter disbelief when I went back to the "word" to find it was all gone! Here comes the confession. I was angry. Real angry! And what was worse I blamed the disappearance of the word on my dear husband. I said, "If I hadn't stopped to call you this wouldn't have happened." Needless to say he was shattered. As I sat doing this task for him I continued to seethe and the body language was so evident. To compound matters, for some "unknown" reason I just could not log onto the website I needed to complete the task I had promised. I even called a friend to asked her to try to see if she could log on to the site but she couldn't either.

You can imagine my state by now. I am angry and I am frustrated and I am achieving nothing. Eventually Lincoln calmly said, "Don't bother to do it anymore. I'll do it myself." Now that didn't make me feel too happy either, but then he added, "The word of the day is good. Reading your Bible and sharing the word is great, but if you don't live it then it is pointless." At that moment it hit me like a ton of bricks.

Two friends, with whom I also share the word, came by to visit me at the same time and when they enquired after him I confessed that I had upset him. NOW I know that I had also grieved the Holy Spirit. I had to admit, "I see why the word of the day could not go out because my behaviour was directly opposite to what I had intended to share, "Put on the LOG, the Light of God," It was a most timely lesson and I apologised to Lincoln right then and there before my friends and told God I accepted His rebuke.

I then started to cry and had to walk away. I have to admit I've been crying since I started to write this as well. But I am comforted in these words from Job 5:17 *"Happy is the one whom God corrects; so do not despise the discipline of the Lord."* and Hebrews 12: 5- 6 *"My son do not make light of the Lord's discipline, and do not lose heart when he rebukes you, because the Lord disciplines the one He loves, and HE chastens everyone HE accepts as HIS son."* Verse 8 states *"If we are not disciplined then we are not true sons and daughters at all."*

Verses 10-11,

> *"God disciplines us for our good, in order that we may share in His holiness. No discipline seems pleasant at the time, but painful. Later on, however, it produces a harvest of righteousness and peace for those who have been trained by it."*

I am truly sorry for my actions but I also know that *"There is now no condemnation for those who are in Christ Jesus, who do not live according to the sinful failure but according to the Spirit"* (Romans 8:1).

I went on to happily complete the task I had promised to do - and would you believe it? There was easy access to the website which somehow would not open before. God is truly amazing and loving even when He rebukes us. It is true "Man looks at the outward appearance, but God looks at the heart." So BE on your guard and accept God's chastening.

15

ODD

Imagine you are all dressed up to go out and you reach for a pair of shoes and put them on. Then you look at yourself in the mirror and to your dismay, you are wearing two different shoes. Funny? Yes! The expected immediate reaction should be to find the other matching shoe to one of the ones on your feet so that you have two shoes that match. There would be very little point, though, in switching one shoe for another that still didn't match. I don't think you would dare go out to your function dressed in your best with a pair of mismatched shoes, (unless of course you are a bit on the crazy side). Imagine the sneers and the stares you'd get. People would be talking about it and you for a while.

Once you set out on your journey it's not like you can hide the error you have made, the error you became aware of, but you refused to address. The honest mistake which initially seemed funny, because it was ignored, might not seem so funny anymore. It could be humiliating and the only one you can blame for it is YOURSELF.

In 1 Samuel 15:3 God instructed Saul through the prophet Samuel to, "*Attack the Amalekites and to totally destroy everything that belongs to them.*" The Amalekites were to be punished for what they had done to the Israelites on their journey from Egypt. Saul immediately sought to follow through with the instructions he was given. However he only did so partially. He spared the king and he kept back the best livestock because he was unwilling to destroy them completely.

This made God angry and he expresses His regret in verse 11, "*I regret that I have made Saul king, because he has turned away from me and has not carried out my instructions.*" What was worse was the fact that Saul tried to hide what he had done from Samuel, the prophet, when he was confronted. Saul greets Samuel in verse 13 by saying, *"I have carried out the Lord's instructions."*

Unfortunately Saul did not warn the sheep and cattle, that he had taken, to be quiet because they started bleating and lowing. When his disobedience was discovered, Saul tried to justify it by saying that the soldiers (not him) brought back the best livestock to, *"Sacrifice to the Lord, but we totally destroyed the rest."*

In response, in verse 22 Samuel asks Saul,

> *"Does the Lord delight in burnt offerings and sacrifices as much as obeying the Lord?"* Then the prophet adds, *"To obey is better than sacrifice, and to heed is better than the fat of rams. For rebellion is like the sin of divination (witchcraft) and arrogance like the evil of idolatry. Because you have rejected the word of the Lord, he has rejected you as king"* (verse 23).

As a result of his failure to obey God completely, Saul lost his kingship and his kingdom.

Obeying God is not always the easiest thing to do but it is the best. I had to eat two good doses of humble pie on Friday and Saturday and it hurt, but I have to say that today I am better off as a result. So the word for you today is Obey, Don't Delay! Listen to what God is telling you and just do it! Be blessed.

16

Be A DOG Christian!

They say that a dog is a man's best friend. If you know anything about them you know that they are loveable, loyal, devoted and will guard their owners and their property well, even to the point of death. They are so trustworthy that many are trained as guide dogs for those who are partially or totally blind. What an awesome responsibility!

Many a story is told of dogs rushing into burning buildings, or jumping into rivers to save loved ones. They don't give it a second thought. Sadly though, sometimes they may perish as a result. In some cases where they have failed to save their loved ones they are known to stay next to the body until rescuers/recoverers arrive.

Interestingly enough, there are all types of dogs - Germany shepherds, Saint Bernards, cocker spaniels, terriers, Chihuahuas, bulldogs, dashunds, poodles, pit bulls, akitas - and the list can go on and on and though some have immense strength and some are puny they all have common weaponry - their bark and their bite! The bark of a small dog may not be as loud as that of a large one and its teeth may not be as big or sharp, but if threatened, both bark and bite can be used very effectively and a dog's bite is not the most pleasant of experiences! Dogs are so valued that owners will erect statues in their memory and even go as far as dying and leaving a share of or an entire estate for them!

One night I went to visit a friend. When I reached the door I stepped over, what I thought was a furry cat, lying in the doorway. When I was ready to leave, however, I came to the awful realization that it was NOT a cat but a dog! He started barking and I stayed rooted to the spot. Although I was allowed to enter, leaving was not so easy. I was obviously being viewed as a threat and the dog was

31

determined to keep me at bay and guard his home. My friend immediately came to my assistance and restrained the dog so that I could return to my car.

This memory reminds me of our relationship with God. His ultimate aim is to keep us safe from our common enemy, the devil. It is for this reason that He sent His Son, Jesus. We are reminded in John 10: 10 that, *"The thief comes only to steal and kill and destroy; I [Jesus] have come that they may have life and have it to the full."*

God continues to do everything to protect His creation. Like the proverbial watchdog He watches over us, He protects us and as an ultimate demonstration of His love and devotion He sacrificed His only Son, Jesus, for us. John 15:13 states, *"Greater love has no one than this: to lay down one's life for one's friends."* But what can we do in return, to show our gratitude to Him? We, too, should have that DOG-like attitude, Let God be first in our lives. Defend Him to the end. Stay with him for as long as it takes. Be loyal! Don't be tempted away by false doctrines!

Jesus states in John 14:6, that He is *"The way and the truth and the life. No one comes to the Father except through [him],"* and in James 1: 17 we are again reminded that, *"Every good and perfect gift is from above, coming down from the Father of the heavenly lights, who does not change like shifting shadows."*

We are warned in 2 Timothy 3:13, however, that in the last days, *"Evildoers and impostors will go from bad to worse, deceiving and being deceived,"* and so we need to guard ourselves against this and we can accomplish this by being a DOG - "Devoted Only to God"- Christian so that we can share in the great eternal reward He has promised us. Have a devoted day!

17

Don't Forget that PIN!

Despite the fact that pins come in all types, shapes and sizes - common, brass, safety, small, medium, large - they are an essential "tool" in any home, school or organisation. Though they may be small, they really shouldn't be regarded as insignificant. When my son was a baby years ago, he wore disposal diapers known as "Pampers" at night, while during the day he wore cloth diapers which I fastened securely with two large diaper pins.

The pins served to keep the diaper firmly in place and to keep any load it carried there as well! Of course a plastic pants was also added! The pins though were not ordinary pins but they had a safety catch that would prevent them from popping open and accidentally sticking my son.

Have you ever gotten dressed and then noticed a stray thread and started to pull on it? If you have ever made that mistake you would know that once you start pulling it, the once neatly stitched area will quickly begin to unravel and will soon be hanging loose. In the absence of a needle and thread, a safety pin is the next best thing to repair the damage. One or more of them discreetly fastened on the inside of the garment will do the trick and "voila!" you have an instant repair job.

This can be done effectively for hems, sleeves, skirts or trousers. Any needle worker (seamstress) or tailor will tell you that his/her kit is incomplete without a generous helping of pins. Just as we use safety pins to rescue us from temporary wardrobe malfunctions so we need spiritual support as well. In our lives we need to remember that PIN, that Prayer Is Necessary. This direct communication with God should be an integral part of our spiritual support system. It is like a safety net against the plans and plots of the devil. Mark 11:24 emphasizes that, *"Whatever, you ask for in prayer, believe that you have received it, and it will be yours."* But just like how one pin is sometimes never enough to get the job done, we need several prayers. Colossians 4:2 emphasizes that you should, *"Devote yourselves to prayer, being watchful and thankful."*

Whatever the circumstance, whatever the need, however big or small, we can take it to God in prayer and expect an answer. James 4:2 teaches us that, *"You do not have because you do not ask God."* Later on in James 5:16, we are told that, *"The prayer of a righteous person is powerful and effective."* In the same way therefore that we may need several pins to keep sections of an article of clothing in place we need daily prayers to support ourselves and others.

1 Thessalonians 5:17 instructs us to, *"Pray continually."* So with that in mind, don't start your day without doing it, don't go through the day without it and don't neglect it before going to sleep. If you really want to see God move powerfully in your life cover each moment and each situation with prayer and don't forget that PIN. Don't forget that Prayer Is Necessary!

18

Own That LOT!

One Friday night some friends and I organized a staff get-together to mark the end of the school year. It was a time for colleagues to get together to socialize - to eat, drink, dance and be merry. The function also doubled as a farewell for some of the staff who would not be returning in the new school year. After a series of meetings, the organizing committee had everything (well, almost everything) in place.

One of our friends thought it would be a great (and a funny) idea to present each person who would be leaving the island with a good piece of Cayman "real estate". Now if you know anything about land lots they can be expensive! Whether they are big or small, purchasing one can set you back financially.

Despite this fact, however, one of the goals of many persons is to own their own lot and though it may mean paying a mortgage over several years, the end result is well worth it. It's yours! You don't have to pay rent, (which they say is "dead" money). You can build on it. You can bequeath some or all of it to your children or you can sell it, usually for more than you bought it for. I wouldn't, however, recommend that my former colleagues who are leaving try that though!

Now back to the night of the social. As the leavers' names were called they were asked to come forward and they each received their little "lot". It comprised a zip lock bag with some rocks in it! The original plan was to give them some sand. We had not managed to do that, but quick thinking on the part of my friend that night led us to discreetly scoop some rocks up from the yard and prepare each real estate package! People thought it was hilarious.

Don't think for a moment though that that was all they got, as we also presented them with special personalized gifts, which we expect they would treasure a whole lot more! I heard that one recipient really treasured the first gift - the lot that they got.

In life we each need to strive for our own LOT. God is so good to us, but often we only see the problems which the devil presents and we spend so much time complaining that we are blinded to God's everlasting faithfulness and goodness.

Throughout the book of Psalms the psalmist David encourages us to be thankful: Psalm 100:4 tells us to *"Enter his gates with thanksgiving and His courts with praise; give thanks to him and praise his name."* Again in Psalm 107:1, David orders us to, *"Give thanks to the Lord, for He is good; His love endures forever."* Are you reading this? Then give God thanks, for it is He who has woken you up and given you the gift of sight and the list of things to be thankful for can be endless.

More importantly, God loves it when we thank Him, when we pause to express our appreciation for each blessing. Just think how we feel when we give someone something and they don't say thanks. God enjoys hearing us say "Thank you," too. Let us follow the psalmist's advice in Psalm 69: 30 *"I will praise God's name in song and glorify him with thanksgiving. This will please the Lord more than an ox, more than a bull with its horns and hooves."* So own that LOT - Life of Thanksgiving - for nothing compares to it.

Be thankful.

19

There Is A VIP and There Is A VIP

Oh how times have surely changed. We have all types of gadgets designed to make our lives better, but has life really improved? Many will say, "Yes" and refer to it as "progress". I agree somewhat but spell it differently though, "POORgress." We have invented washing machines to make washing easier and they have, but many no longer know how to wash by hand. There is the calculator which has replaced, it seems, mental math. No need to learn those number facts and times tables anymore!

Then there's the computer. Complete with spell check, it's no wonder that knowing how to spell correctly is slowly becoming an obsolete ability. Finally, there is the smart phone! What a great invention! If it weren't for it I sure wouldn't have broadcast this message in the way that I did prior to writing this book.

In days gone by I would have needed a loudspeaker or a radio or TV to broadcast my message! While texting, replete with its abbreviations - BFF, GM, LOL, OMG - has also sought to improve communication, at times it really is a struggle to understand what these tech babies are saying. Sadly, spelling has suffered and personally I don't think many people really know how to spell anymore. The education system isn't immune either, as educators now use the following abbreviations BFL, SEN (now SEND), AFL, EOY, EYP and there are lots more too! But if you don't know what they mean - and I am pretty sure that some of you reading this don't either - then what's the point?

How has communication improved? In time past it was the rule - it still is but people have ignored it completely - to spell out in full the acronym the first time it is being used and then abbreviate it for each subsequent use. With that said, my message is "there's a VIP and there's a VIP".

We were created to worship God and He delights in our praises. Psalm 22:3 states, "*But you are holy, O you who inhabit the praises of Israel,*" and in Psalm 33:1 we read, "*Sing joyful to the Lord, you righteous; it is fitting for the upright to praise Him.*"

But what is our praise like? Is it half-hearted? Are there times we don't feel like praising? It really matters not how we feel because God commands us to praise Him and our praises should be coming from a grateful heart for all He has done, continues to do and will do.

In 1 Chronicles 16:8-10 we are exhorted to,

> "*Give praise to the Lord, proclaim His name; make known among the nations what He has done. Sing to Him, sing praise to Him; tell of His wonderful acts. Glory in His holy name; let the hearts of those who seek the Lord rejoice.*"

Praising God then, is clearly a command and we are not only expected to do it, we need to do it joyfully. Psalm 100:1 orders us to, "*Make a joyful noise unto the Lord, all the earth,*" and in Psalm 150: 3-6, we are told to do it WHOLEHEARTEDLY.

> "*Praise Him with the sounding of the trumpet, praise him with the harp and the lyre, praise Him with tambourine and dancing, praise Him with the strings and flute, praise Him with the clash of cymbals, praise him with resounding cymbals. Let everything that has breath praise the Lord.*"

Just as important as praising our VIP, God, is the fact that there is also a VIP - Victory In Praise. 2 Samuel 22:4 and Psalm 18:3 tell us, "*I called to the Lord, who is worthy of praise, and I have been saved from my enemies.*" This is reiterated in Psalm 8:2 "*Through the praise of children and infants you have established a stronghold against your enemies, to silence the foe and the avenger.*" When we praise in faith the walls in our lives will come tumbling down just like the walls of Jericho did (See Joshua 6).

Still doubtful about what praise can do? Read 2 Chronicles 20:21-22 where, following God's instruction, King Jehoshaphat commanded the people to sing and praise God and when they did God set up ambushes against their enemies and they won the battle.

So remember that there is a VIP and there is a VIP - Victory In Praise for a Very Important Person! Have a praising day!

20

Just ASK

It's amazing how you can receive something which you asked for but not really expected to get! Sounds a bit strange, doesn't it? Some time ago I was chatting online with a friend and told him to inform his wife that I would be stopping by to pay her a visit before going off on holiday. He advised me to pass by soon so that I could get some of her bread pudding.

Unfortunately I don't eat bread pudding and I told him that, adding that I wouldn't mind having apple pie, instead ending the message with "LOL", because I was joking. Imagine my very pleasant surprise when two days later while talking to my friend I found out that she had indeed made the apple pie and was wondering when I intended to pass by for it.

On reflection this is sometimes like our relationship with God. We ask or He offers but we don't expect to receive so we lose out on some of the blessings He has in store for us. In Luke 11: 9-10 Jesus says,

> *"Ask and it will be given to you; seek and you will find; knock and the door will be opened to you. For everyone who asks receives; the one who seeks finds; and to the one who knocks, the door will be opened."*

In jest, I asked my friend for apple pie and she made it, but you know if I don't go and eat that apple pie the purpose for which it was made would not be fulfilled. It would almost be as if she would have made it in vain and she might naturally feel disappointed.

In Ephesians 3:20 the apostle Paul identifies God as being able to do *"Immeasurably more than all we ask or imagine, according to the power that is at work in us."* That power comes through the Holy Spirit which Jesus first promised to His disciples in Acts 1:4 when he instructs them, *"Do not leave Jerusalem, but wait for the gift my Father promised,"* with the assurance in verse 8 that they, *"Will receive power when the Holy Spirit comes on [them]."*

In the same way my friend was willing to satisfy my desire and made the effort to make that apple pie for me, Jesus informs us in Luke 11:13 that God, our Father knows how to give even better gifts: *"If [we] know how to give good gifts to [our] children* (and by extension our friends) *how much more will [our] Father in heaven give the Holy Spirit to those who ask him!"* We will not run the risk of being disappointed though, because God does not lie and in Psalm 84:11, He promises us that, *"No good thing does He withhold from those whose walk is blameless."* Our task, therefore, is simple: Just ASK - Ask, Seek, Knock, but do so expecting to receive and you will never be disappointed.

21

Get to STEPping

A popular Chinese proverb says, "The journey of a thousand miles begins with one step." Any person who has ever run a marathon will tell you that they did not just wake up one morning and decide to take part in the gruelling 26 mile event to be held on that same day. They may wake up and decide they will compete in one but if they are smart enough they also know that they need to spend hours, weeks, months and maybe years, training hard, both physically and mentally BEFORE they take that first step.

The course is not only long; it is tough as well, but still runners plod on, step after step, many times under scorching sun or through pouring rain. Some may slow down to grab water from one of several stops along the way, some may be forced to walk in between but they maintain their focus and when it is over there is a sense of accomplishment for each runner, who reaches that finishing line. Some may finish strongly while others may only stumble or literally crawl over the line, but for each one who manages to complete the course, there is the satisfaction of being able to demonstrate the mental and physical fortitude required to do so. They have made it!

The Christian walk is no different. The road we travel on is rough and there are challenges along the way but we need to get to STEPping, Staying True and Enduring the Pain. In 2 Chronicles 15:7 we are told, "*But as for you, be strong and do not give up, for your work will be rewarded.*" Sometimes we are tempted to stop and give in to the rigours of this life but let us be guided by Galatians 6: 9, "*Let us not become weary in doing good, for at the proper time we will reap a harvest if we do not give up.*" Where will we get that strength from? From God himself! "*But they that wait upon the Lord shall renew their strength. They shall mount up with wings as eagles; they shall run and not be weary, they shall walk and not be faint"* (Isaiah 40:31). So get to STEPping - Staying True and Enduring the Pain and, *"Let us run with perseverance the race marked out for us, fixing our eyes on Jesus, the pioneer and perfecter of faith"* (Hebrews 12:1-2).

Have a persevering day!

22

Hands Up

I watch a lot of westerns. Sometimes during a gun battle, the leader of one group, after analysing the situation, will realize that the odds are stacked strongly against his band of men, and so he'll say to his partners, "Hold your fire, men!" and to the other group he'll shout, "We're coming out. Don't shoot!" In response, their opponents, just to ensure that it's not a trick, will respond with, "Throw out/down your guns and come out with your hands in the air!" The agreement is honoured, group one surrenders and they are then taken captive by the second group.

As Christians we need to put our hands up too. When we do so we are demonstrating to God that we are surrendering ourselves to him and He will then take it from there.

In 1 Samuel 17: 45 while standing facing the taunting and intimidating giant, Goliath, David the little shepherd boy, against whom the odds appeared to be stacked, shouts confidently, *You come against me with sword and spear and javelin, but I come against you in the name of the Lord Almighty,"* adding in verse 47, *"All those gathered here will know that it is not by sword or spear that the Lord saves, for the battle is the Lord's and He will give all of you into our hands."* The end result?

David went on to defeat the once mighty Goliath with a small stone and Goliath's countrymen, the Philistines turned and ran, pursued by the Israelites. We too can defeat the giants in our lives. We just need to put our hands up, not in surrender to the enemy but like antennae to God and let Him take it from there. The songwriter says:

All to Jesus, I surrender;
All to Him I freely give.

I will ever love and trust Him,
In His presence daily live.

I surrender all,
I surrender all
All to thee my blessed Saviour
I surrender all.[4]

So, Hands up!

---

[4] Judson W. Van DeVenter, *I Surrender All*

23

The Real McCoy[5]

The true origin of this idiom is debatable. Some people believe it is a corruption of the Scottish word Mackay while others think it was named after an engineer called Elijah McCoy, who invented an oil drip cup. The term was used to distinguish his invention from fake cups which were sometimes used as substitutes. Regardless of the true origin, however, when used, the expression refers to something or someone that is real or genuine and not fake.

Sometimes crafty criminals would successfully use imitation firearms while committing a crime. The fear instilled by the "gunman" and the trauma caused are just as real as if the weapon were real. If caught the consequences for perpetrators are just as severe as if they were using the real McCoy. Though an imitation weapon is essentially harmless, potential victims who are staring down the barrel of that gun have no way of knowing and would be advised to treat it as though it were real.

Jesus Is the real McCoy and we need not doubt His authenticity or fear that He cannot accomplish what He says He will do. In John 14:6 He states emphatically that He is, "The *way, and the truth, and the life. No one comes to the Father except through [Him].*" He makes it very easy to do so as well as we are told in Acts 16:31 to "*Believe in the Lord Jesus, and you will be saved, you and your house.*" In John 10:10-11 Jesus makes His mission clear, by stating, "*I am come that they may have life, and have it to the full,*" and He has achieved this by, "*Laying down His life for* [us, His] *sheep.*"

Jesus is indeed the Real McCoy.

_____

[5] Accessed 6th July 2015 Wikipedia Internet Reference

24

Be A Bee

What do you think about when you hear about bees? Stings? Honey? Hives? All three are synonymous with them. Bees live in hives, where they make and store honey, but they will use stings as a defense mechanism if they feel threatened.

Some years ago as I was driving merrily along a local road with my windows down, a bee flew right into the car. At that moment I think I became a serious contender for the fastest person to stop a car and exit. I jumped out and tried to swat the bee but it flew off before I could perform my dastardly deed. Interestingly enough now years later honey is my first sweetener of choice.

But what is so fascinating about bees? Well, first of all they go from flower to flower (the brighter the better the attraction) collecting pollen and sipping nectar, which they store in their throats until they return to their hives where they turn it into honey. The plants in turn depend on bees to spread the pollen which helps the former to reproduce.

Although thousands upon thousands of bees live in colonies or hives they come together effectively working productively for the good of the hive. The bees have a model communication system[6]. As Christians we would do well to emulate them.

In Matthew 9:37 Jesus warns us that, "*The harvest is plentiful but the workers are few*." We are God's ears, eyes, hands, feet and voice. He is depending on us to help Him accomplish His mission of winning the lost. We must share the Gospel - good news - with others.

---

[6] Accessed 7th July 2015 *Wikipedia Internet Reference*

The apostle Paul encourages us in Romans 1:16 to do it boldly, "*For I am not ashamed of the gospel, because it is the power of God that brings salvation to everyone who believes: first to the Jew, then to the Gentile.*" In Mark 2: 17 Jesus emphasizes that, "*It is not the healthy who need a doctor, but the sick,*" reminding us that, "*[He] did not come to call the righteous but sinners.*" "*God did not send Jesus into the world to condemn the world, but to save it through Him*" (John 3:17). The world is a mighty big place but with a collective effort on our part we can be organized, productive and effective just like a bee. So Be a Bee!

25

Lazarus, Come Forth! Sit and Wait!

I was not sure how to entitle this message so take your pick: Lazarus, Come Forth! or Sit and Wait!

Oh what a day and night I had yesterday! Absolutely incredible!

1 Corinthians 1:25 tells us that, "*The foolishness of God is wiser than human wisdom and the weakness of God is stronger than human strength.*" My husband, Lincoln and I are currently staying at a hotel in Miami. It was the first time we had been here. For us it is customary to buy on line and have the packages sent to the hotel. Would you believe that despite him checking at the reception early in the morning and alerting them that we were expecting items, when the items came they refused to take them. As a result they were sent back to the shippers! The excuse: My FIRST name was not on the reservation. Needless to say I was upset and I did not accept their reasoning at all. I asked to see the manager who explained that it was a trainee on the job and he agreed with me that the logical thing for her to have done was to check the last name on the guest list and place a call to the room. He apologized profusely and then offered us the night FREE. He also called Amazon on my behalf and let me speak to the reps there. It is interesting to note that the items were not even for either of us! Later I was forced to reorder them.

Later in the day, I was expecting a Skype call and of all the times for the connections to act up that was the time. Earlier when we were at the front desk Lincoln had mentioned to the manager that I was expecting this call and he had offered to walk me over to the business centre of a nearby hotel to ensure I wouldn't miss it. Now I needed to call in that favour and I did, but I was still unsuccessful.

It is interesting to note that UPS arrived with a package for my best friend at the same time I was at reception. If that had not been received it would have been impossible for it to be reordered and sent back before my departure. Back to the Skype call - the often reliable Internet was having a field day with me. I sent an email supposedly to the person who had informed me of the Skype call, only to realize later that I had sent it to MYSELF! With time approaching I started getting a bit anxious.

I tried to send a WhatsApp message to someone else in authority but it did not go through and of course there was no response. Just as I had given up on this call (I actually started to undress) my phone rang and when I answered I was told by the caller that she had sent an invite to my husband's Skype address which I had used as an alternative. We quickly accepted and the call was made shortly after.

Fast forward to later that night and after dinner we go to Walmart. We exit the store at around 10:45, load the car and I attempt to start it. Nothing, absolutely nothing happened. We sought help from a fellow shopper but still nothing. Then things got real interesting or unbelievable. We called the road side assistance number listed on the rental agreement, not once, not twice but a few times and each time we went through the same procedure: name, licence number, expiration etc.

We were told they would send someone in the next hour. When the time was up we called again only to be told 30 mins more. The guy eventually showed up at 12:50! By this time Walmart is closed (they don't all offer 24hr service we discovered) and besides the cleaners, we are the only ones left in the carpark. The guy, who has come all the way from Fort Lauderdale and who I am convinced is only a professional battery charger tries to jump start the car, only to discover that this was not a battery problem at all. We call again only to be told that we would need to wait until a wrecker came. The wrecker would bring a replacement car, but it would take another 90 minutes. Our "battery charger" leaves at 1:00. We sit and we wait, because we have been told that should we leave the car, it would be treated as abandonment! Then we call some more and each time we are calmly told, "We apologise and we know how you feel. Thank you for choosing . . ." I really don't want to hear it.

At last the wrecker arrives at 2:45 in the morning with a nice shiny blue Hyundai Accent, similar to the one we saw and refused when we took the first rental car. Now here's the "best" bit. He gets behind the wheel of the first car, puts the key in the ignition and turns it. To our (the night security is on the scene by now) complete bewilderment, it starts. To say we were in awe is a definite understatement. Guess what the wrecker's name was? Lazaro which is Spanish for Lazarus!

As we drove along in our new ride with a full tank of gas we couldn't help but marvel at what had just happened.

God certainly,

> "Chose the foolish things of this world to shame the wise; God chose the weak things of the world to shame the strong. [He] chose the lowly things of this world and the despised things - and the things that are not - to nullify the things that are, so that no one may boast before Him" (1 Corinthians 1:27-28).

We concluded that this was God's personal lesson to us about sitting and waiting - not on people, not on the Internet, not on Roadside Rescues but on Him. The situation may seem dead and the signs may indicate it is hopeless but God is faithful and He WILL show up when we need Him. Singer Nicole C Mullen puts it so well when she says "When we call on Jesus all things are possible."

Sit and Wait on God and in due time He will say, "Lazarus Come forth."

26

911. What's Your Emergency?

That's the voice of the operator as he/she answers the emergency hotline. People will call with any issue that they deem urgent even if some things seem quite frivolous. I am sure that during training, potential operators or tele-communicators to use modern day jargon, are trained that they must act professionally at all times and each case of emergency is to be treated as just as important as the other. They must treat callers politely and use all their skills as effectively as possible to get help for the person who needs it desperately and to get that help quickly.

However, before help is dispatched operators need to engage in a Q and A session. They need your name, your date of birth, your address, your actual location and more. Though this can take up valuable time it is a necessity. Although in most cases the caller or the person on whose behalf the call is being made will receive the assistance sought and there is a happier ending, sometimes sadly the ending is not so happy at all.

Thanks be to God, Jesus is not like the 911 tele-communicator but God does have His own styled 911 communication centre. All calls are answered promptly and once you follow the advice He gives you there is ALWAYS the happiest ending. Check it out in Psalm 91. One thing is for sure, with Him all help is guaranteed.

Psalm 91

> [1] *He that dwells in the secret place of the most High shall abide under the shadow of the Almighty.* [2] *I will say of the Lord, He is my refuge and my fortress: my God; in Him will I put my trust.* [3] *Surely He shall deliver you from the snare of the fowler, and from*

the noisome pestilence.[4.] *He shall cover you with His feathers, and under His wings shall you trust: His truth shall be your shield and buckler.*[5.] *You shall not be afraid for the terror by night; nor for the arrow that flies by day;*[6.] *Nor for the pestilence that walks in darkness; nor for the destruction that wastes at noonday.* [7.] *A thousand shall fall at your side and ten thousand at your right hand; but it shall not come near you.*[8.] *Only with your eyes shall you behold and see the reward of the wicked.*[9.] *Because you have made the Lord, which is my refuge, even the most High, your habitation;*[10.] *There shall no evil befall you, neither shall any plague come nigh your dwelling.*[11.] *For He shall give His angels charge over you, to keep you in all your ways.*[12.] *They shall bear you up in their hands, less you dash your foot against a stone.*[13.] *You shall tread upon the lion and adder: the young lion and the dragon shall you trample under feet.*[14.] *Because he has set his love on me, therefore will I deliver him: I will set him on high, because he has known My name.*[15.] *He shall call upon Me, and I will answer him: I will be with him in trouble; I will deliver him, and honour him.*[16.] *With long life will I satisfy him, and show him my salvation.*

911, what's your emergency?

27

Grab Those Shades!

Summer is very much here and the sun is not only hot it is very bright as well. Ever been out on a bright sunny day and you have had to squint to try to see? Usually happens when you are not wearing shades. Because of this many people will not go out until they have grabbed their sunglasses, because not only do they look trendy but they also offer special protection against the UV rays of the sun.

In my home we have taken extra precautions against the heat of the sun. We have tinted our windows and have also installed venetian blinds. The effect is phenomenal. Though the days are terribly hot the heat inside is significantly reduced.

In like manner Christians need to grab their spiritual shades to protect themselves. Ephesians 6:11 tells us to, *Put on the full armour of God, so that you can take your stand against the devil's schemes."* The apostle Paul emphasizes the need to do so again in verse 13, *"Therefore put on the full armour of God, so that when the day of evil comes, you may be able to stand your ground, after you have done everything."* There can be no denying that we are in the "evil day" but victory is assured if we make sure we grab these "shades" which are identified in verses 14-18:

1. The belt of truth
2. The breastplate of righteousness
3. Feet shod with the preparation of the gospel of peace
4. The shield of faith
5. The helmet of salvation

6. The sword of the spirit which is the word of God and

7. Prayer in the Spirit

We must clad ourselves fully each day so that we can avoid the devil's attacks, defeat him when he comes and tear down every stronghold that he seeks to establish. 2 Corinthians 10:3 informs us that, *"The weapons of our warfare are not carnal, but mighty through God to the pulling down of strongholds;"*

Then can we truly say, "My future is so bright I have to wear shades!"[7]

Grab those shades!

---

[7] Accessed 26th July 2015 *FaceBook Internet Reference*

28
DIY

Do it yourself is one of those crazes that is growing in popularity. In an effort to save money many people are opting to complete a myriad of household projects themselves.

Whether it is erecting shelving, installing carpet, plumbing, tiling or some other type of masonry or carpentry, persons with little or no expertise or experience are taking on the challenge. They use the step by step instructions, the manual provided or watch a how to video to guide them along. While some do-it-yourselfers must be commended for their efforts some projects have been known to be total flops. When this happens persons are left with no other choice but to call in an expert to get the job done. I don't know of too many artisans who have refused jobs which amateurs have started but failed.

In Luke 15:11-17, the prodigal son asks for his inheritance and goes off and spends it all. When he comes to the end of his rope and comes to the realization that he has failed this project he decides to return home to the safety and security of his father's home.

In verses 18 and 19, he states,

> "I will arise and go to my father, and will say unto him, Father, I have sinned against heaven, and before you, and am no more worthy to be called your son: make me as one of your hired servants."

He acknowledges that he has failed and needs help.

He makes the choice to return to the safety of his father's home even if it is as a servant. Verse 20 tells us that, "*He arose and came to his father,"* who has been anxiously awaiting his return. His father spies him from a distance and runs to meet him and has a celebration to mark his return. *"But when he was a great way off, his father saw him, and had compassion and ran and fell on his neck and kissed him."*

Sometimes we condemn the son for demanding his inheritance and wasting it but we need to commend him for having the presence of mind to recognize the error of his ways, to repent and ask for forgiveness. We learn from 1 John 1:9 that, *"If we confess our sins He (God) is faithful and just to forgive us our sins, and to cleanse us from all unrighteousness."* In response to Joshua's command in Joshua 24:15 to, *"Choose whom they will serve,"* the people are adamant that they will serve God,

> *"Far be it from us to forsake the Lord to serve other gods It was the Lord our God Himself who brought us and our parents up out of Egypt . . . and performed those great signs before our eyes. He protected us on our entire journey. . . . And the Lord drove out before us all the nations. . . . We too will serve the Lord, because He is our God"* (Verses 16-18).

So don't do it yourself or your way. Do It Yahweh's.

29

IF

The word "if" is one of the smallest words in the English language but it is one with huge significance. Many people go through life filled with what ifs. If I had not done this or that then I wouldn't be in this position now. If you had told me I might have . . . If I had known I would/wouldn't have . . . If you really cared then you would . . . and so on and so on. God also deals in what ifs. In Revelation 3:20 He says, "*Behold, I stand at the door and knock. IF anyone hears my voice and opens the door, I will come in and eat with that person, and they with me.*"

Again in James 1:5 we are told, "*IF any of you lacks wisdom, you should ask God, who gives generously to all without finding fault, and it will be given to you.*" 2 Chronicles 7:14 adds,

> "*IF my people who are called by my name, will humble themselves and pray and seek my face and turn from their wicked ways, then I will hear from heaven, and I will forgive their sin and will heal their land.*"

Everyone is longing for deliverance from their troubles and sometimes it seems that instead of getting better things are getting worse. But rest assured there is deliverance in Jesus but before it is realized there must be repentance.

Whenever we repent before God He forgives us and brings healing and restoration. His conditions are clear and simple yet so fulfilling. IF you choose to, "*Seek first the kingdom of God, and His righteousness all these things shall be added unto you* (Matthew 6:33).

2 Corinthians 5:17 explains that, "*IF anyone is in Christ He is a new creature: old things are passed away; behold all things are become new.*" We

are also told in Revelation 20:15, however, what will happen if we refuse God's invitation and choose to remain separated from Him, "*And whosoever was not found in the book of life was cast into the lake of fire.*" We do not need to suffer or perish unduly because of the final IF, realized on the cross of Calvary when Jesus paid the price for all our sins and exclaimed, "*It's Finished*!"

Because Jesus paid our debt in full we can face each circumstance without being intimidated, confident that we are not fighting for victory but FROM a position OF victory just because IF - It's Finished!

30

I Spy

Regardless to the type of spying involved - industrial, nuclear, military, national or international - what is always most disconcerting with this clandestine activity is the fact that information which is regarded by leaders of organisations or countries as top secret, has been compromised by someone who has managed to cunningly infiltrate a system and gained unauthorised access.

The threats involved in espionage are so potentially severe and the risks so great that if caught, guilty parties could face the death penalty. It is no wonder therefore why spies will charge inordinate amounts of money - thousands and even millions of dollars - in exchange for the handing over of documents considered sacred by potential victims. Leaders will often go to extraordinary lengths to protect a company's or a nation's secrets for as long as possible, ensuring also that information is guarded by a select few.

Despite the best efforts though, unscrupulous persons may just manage to weave themselves in and when this happens panic sets in as danger looms.

The devil and his imps are a type of infiltrator. In the beginning when God created Adam and Eve He gave them authority and dominion over everything. Genesis 1:27-28,

> "So God created man in His own image, in the image of God created He him; male and female created He them. And God blessed them, and God said unto them, Be fruitful and multiply, and replenish the earth, and subdue it: and have dominion over the fish of the sea, and over the fowl of the air, and over every living thing that moveth upon the earth."

Through deception, however, Satan attempted to steal this authority and dominion, but all was recovered with Jesus' death on the cross.

As believers in Christ we therefore have this authority, but many of us act as though we are not aware of this powerful fact. Hosea 4:6 tells us, "*My people are destroyed for lack of knowledge.*"

According to Bishop Duncan Williams in his book, Binding the Strong Man[8] "[Our] ignorance is the strength of the enemy!" He adds that, "The extent of information that you have about the strategies of the enemy will determine your level of advantage over him." Williams warns that in the same way governments and large organisations utilize much of their resources to acquire information about their adversaries and sometimes their friends, as Christians we would do well to acquire maximum knowledge about the covert operations of our enemy, the devil.

He suggests we need to access the enemy's strategies, gain insight on how to deal with the master spirits which exert their influence in several areas of our lives and acquire ways of identifying evil spirits. Remember Satan's chief goal is to "*Steal, kill and destroy,*" (John 10:10) and our very existence depends on knowing how he and his imps work. We can acquire this knowledge and infiltrate the kingdom of darkness by reading God's blueprint, the Bible. Ephesians 6:12 reminds us that, "*We wrestle not against flesh and blood, but against principalities, against powers, against the rulers of the darkness of this world, against spiritual wickedness in high places.*"

I spy. What do you spy?

---

[8] Bishop Duncan Williams, *Binding the Strong Man,* 2012

31

Watch Out For The Iguanas[9]!

If you know anything about iguanas you know that they are very large lizards, ranging in length from 5 to 6 feet, with scales running down their backs to their tails. Even though they have great vision and can view shapes, shadows, colours and movement at long distances, and have the benefit of a "third eye" on their heads they cannot make out details, just brightness.

Perhaps the best known fact about them is that they are masters of disguise and are often unable to be spotted because of their unique ability to blend into their surroundings, which they use as a defense mechanism against predators. Known as camouflaging this technique is also employed by soldiers on the battlefield to conceal themselves from their enemies. Their aim is to plan a strategic strike at a time known only to them. It is hoped that the element of surprise will catch opponents unaware and hopefully enhance one's chances for victory.

Satan too has the ability to camouflage himself and is a master of disguise. In 2 Corinthians 11:14, we are warned, "*And no wonder; for Satan himself masquerades as an angel of light.*" We must therefore be on the alert at all times so that we are not the victims of surprise attacks by the enemy. Sometimes situations appear innocent and there seems to be little harm in engaging in certain activities. Therein lies the error. 1 Thessalonians 5:22, cautions us to, "*Abstain from all appearance of evil.*" By disguising itself the iguana is just hiding amidst its surroundings. That does not mean that it does not exist, however.

---

[9] Accessed 30th July 2015 *Wikipedia Internet Reference*

We need to follow the advice of 1 Thessalonians 5:6, "*Therefore let us not sleep, as do others; but let us watch and be sober.*"

So watch out for the iguanas!

32

IDK

In this era of texting the title of today's message could very well be translated as "I don't know," but as children of God "IDK" should be taken to mean "I Do Know" and with good reason. 2 Timothy 1:12 tells us, *"For I know whom I have believed, and am persuaded that he is able to keep that which I have committed unto him against that day."*

The Bible is filled with the promises of God and they are aye and amen. If we read the word and become familiar with those promises we can answer unequivocally IDK, I Do Know. I Do Know that . . .

I am fearfully and wonderfully made. Psalm 139:14

God is my refuge and strength, an ever present help in the time of trouble. Psalm 46: 1

God's word will not return to Him void, but shall accomplish what He desires and will achieve the purpose for which He has sent it. Isaiah 55:11

No weapon formed against me shall prosper. Isaiah 54:17

My God shall supply all my needs according to His riches in glory by Christ Jesus. Philippians 4:19

God knows the plans that He has for me. Plans to prosper me and not to harm me, plans to give me hope and a future. Jeremiah 29:11

No good thing will God withhold from me if I walk uprightly. Psalm 84:11

The Lord will keep me from all harm - he will watch over my life; He will watch over my coming and going both now and evermore. Psalm 121:7-8

Goodness and mercy shall follow me all the days of my life.
Psalm 23:6

I have been young and now am old; yet have I never seen the righteous forsaken, nor His seed begging bread. Psalm 37:25

All things work together for good to them that love God, to them who are called according to His purpose. Romans 8:28

Greater is He who is in me than He that is in the world. 1 John 4:4

In due season I shall reap if I faint not. Galatians 6:9

They that wait upon the Lord shall renew their strength. They shall mount up on wings as eagles; they shall run and not be weary, they shall walk and not faint. Isaiah 40:31

If I seek first the kingdom of God and His righteousness all other things shall be added unto me. Matthew 6:33

I can do all things through Christ who strengthens me.
Philippians 4:13

These are but just a few of the myriad of promises which are contained in God's book, the Bible. Search the source for more and add them to this list. Keep telling yourself and others IDK, I Do Know what God says about me and I Do Know what plans He has in store for me. Don't forget to remind the devil as well.

Have a promise-filled day.

33
ASAP

Many times when a request is made persons will add "asap" at the end. By doing this they are intimating that the situation is urgent and a response is needed promptly, "as soon as possible."

Often times we find ourselves in circumstances which so concern us that we need answers and we also need them ASAP. Establishing and maintaining communication with our Heavenly Father is critical to our everyday existence and prayer offers us that direct link.

1 Thessalonians 5:17 advises us to, "*Pray continually,*" while Ephesians 6:18 tells us to "*Pray in the spirit on all occasions with all kinds of prayers and requests.*" We can go to God at any time about anything. Even though God never turns us away, it is always better to be in constant dialogue with Him. Don't wait until a problem arises to start to talk to Him.

Listen to one songwriter's advice:

> *Whisper a prayer in the morning*[10]
> *Whisper a prayer at noon*
> *Whisper a prayer in the evening*
> *To keep your heart in tune.*
>
> *God answers prayer in the morning*
> *God answers prayer at noon*
> *God answers prayer in the evening*
> *So keep your hearts in tune*

So ASAP - Always Say A Prayer.

---

[10] *Whisper a Prayer In the Morning Anonymous* Internet reference, accessed 17th July 2015

34

We Are In Good "PAWS"

A few years ago my husband attended a friend's funeral in Zimbabwe. While there he visited a wild life reserve. According to him, at one point during the tour a lion got up and peered into the vehicle. My husband had his camera in hand, but despite the urgings of the other guys he refused to take a picture. He admitted that he was afraid that the flash would startle the lion which he described as huge, rather formidable and presenting an imposing figure. And he wasn't taking any chances!

A while afterwards I was watching a documentary on lions and got further insight into these amazing creatures. Not only are the adults very large with enormous paws, a blow from one of which can be lethal, but their strength is immeasurable. They can appear docile at times but can also be very intimidating, as my husband experienced. They are also very persistent with excellent staying in power and highly protective. These characteristics make this creature one to be feared. No wonder therefore that the lion is dubbed the "King of the Jungle."

They say a picture is worth a thousand words, and while I was overawed with all of the lion's attributes I did not feel the fear my husband felt because unlike me, who was viewing everything through a screen, he had actually encountered the real thing.

When I consider the above, contrasting descriptions of Jesus and our arch-enemy, Satan come to mind. I view the devil as an impostor, trying to impersonate Jesus. He *prowls around LIKE a roaring lion looking for someone to devour."* (1 Peter 5:8.) Because he isn't the real thing he doesn't have all the attributes of a real lion.

Jesus, on the other hand IS the King of the "jungle." "*He is King of Kings and Lord of Lords*" (Revelation 19:16). He IS NOT LIKE a roaring lion. He IS the conquering Lion of the tribe of Judah (Revelation 5:5).

Just imagine that the one who fights for us is persistent, persevering, loving, fearless, protective, intimidating towards our enemies, omnipotent. No doubt about it. We are in good "paws".

35

Bonfire

I spent my very early years in England. The 5th of November was (and still is) celebrated as Bonfire Night, also referred to as Guy Fawkes[11] Day. Days and sometimes weeks before the actual date, children would carry around the stuffed effigy of a man, dressed in old clothes, repeating the refrain, "Please to remember the 5th of November, Gunpowder treason and plot."

The effigy known as Guy Fox, was due to be burnt on top a bonfire on the 5th and represented Guido Fawkes, who, along with a group of co-conspirators, had attempted to blow up the English Houses of Parliament in the 17th century in an effort to kill King James 1, who was not well-liked by many of his subjects, because of his poor treatment towards them, especially those with differing religious views. If the plot had succeeded, however, many innocent people some of whom were relatives of Fawkes' co-conspirators, would also have lost their lives.

Isn't it "interesting" that people down through the ages continue to commemorate a man who really and truly was nothing more than a terrorist, who was willing to sacrifice many innocent lives just to rid the country/world of one man by blowing up a building and creating a huge bonfire? More "interesting" is the fact that despite masterminding this treasonous plot, Guy Fawkes has been described by some as a "brave man and a gentleman, a faithful friend to the limit of endurance, ready to die for the faith in which he believed." In stark contrast, sacrificing His Son Jesus on the cross of Calvary was God's ultimate demonstration of His love for all mankind. Romans

---

[11] *James I and the Gunpowder Plot a Lady Bird Book,* Lawrence du Garde Peach *1967*

5:8 reminds us, *"But God demonstrates His own love for us in this: While we were still sinners, Christ died for us."*

When Adam sinned, we were all doomed, but Jesus brought life and hope for us all.

Romans 5:18-19 posits,

> [18]*"Consequently, just as one trespass resulted in condemnation for all people, so also one righteous act resulted in justification and life for all people.* [19]*For just as through the disobedience of the one man the many were made sinners, so also through the obedience of the one man the many will be made righteous."*

There is absolutely no comparison between Guy Fawkes and Jesus. Had Guy Fawkes' plot succeeded he would have brought heartache to many. Jesus on the other hand successfully completed his mission and for that we ought all to be eternally grateful and should demonstrate our gratitude each day of each year. Let us always B On Fire for God!

Let us, *"Bless the Lord at all times,"* and let, *"His praise be continually in [our] mouth"* Psalm 34:1.

B On Fire!

36

Hook Up To TOPS

Some years ago, the school I work at, initiated a programme called TOPS, The Opportunities Programme, which was an intervention programme for students with behavioural challenges. The unit was manned by behaviour specialists who worked closely with pupils to try to modify and hopefully eradicate undesirable behavioural patterns which were being exhibited with some regularity. The results were slow in coming and after a while the programme was abandoned. Unfortunately, of course the same problems continued to manifest themselves and other initiatives were implemented with mixed results.

Some well-known and very influential Biblical characters initially had behavioural problems too. Paul who wrote many of the epistles, was once called Saul, a persecutor and killer of Christians. Peter, who later became one of Jesus' most trusted disciples was a foul-mouthed fisherman.

Zacchaeus, once an unscrupulous tax collector, restored much more than he had stolen. In his impatience Abraham, known as the Father of nations, acted rashly and impregnated his wife's maid. Jacob, considered a patriarch of the Israelites was a schemer, a trickster and a liar. The psalmist David was an adulterer and killer. These are but just a few examples.

What is significant about each of these persons, was that they all had an encounter with TOPS. Their opportunities for eventual, long-lasting and effective change, however, were facilitated because they hooked up to a TOPS programme of a different nature. They aligned themselves with The Omnipotent Power Source, God. Theirs was not simply behaviour modification, but it was behaviour remake. Under

God's tutelage we are never the same again. Though they may defy human intellect His strategies are highly effective.

According to Isaiah 55:8 God says, "*My thoughts are not your thoughts, neither are your ways my ways.*" Our role therefore, is simply to, "*Trust in the Lord with all [our] hearts and lean not on [our] own understanding. In all our ways acknowledge Him and He shall direct [our] paths.*" Proverbs 3:5-6. With God at the helm we don't have to fear the "programme or initiative" coming to an abrupt or untimely end and our success is guaranteed. Remember, "*If any man is in Christ he is a new creature: old things are passed away; behold, all things are become as new*" 2 Corinthians 5:17.

There is definitely nothing to lose. So hook up to TOPS - The Omnipotent Power Source - today.

37

FITS

The first time I witnessed someone experience an epileptic seizure, commonly known as the "fits", I was terrified. I was a child in town with my mother and we had stopped to get something to eat. A man next to us had been eating a sandwich when suddenly he fell to the ground and began to twitch uncontrollably while frothing at the mouth. A lady quickly ran to his side and shouted for someone to get a spoon to place between his teeth so that he didn't "swallow" his tongue. I watched as she and another person who had come to his aid tried to prise open his teeth to insert the spoon.

Meanwhile my mum whipped out her bottle of smelling salts and passed it under the man's nose, while someone else rubbed him with Limacol (or Alcolado Glacial). Just as quickly as the attack began it came to an end. The man was totally oblivious to what was going on and when he regained consciousness he was quite shocked to find himself on the ground. After chatting with his helpers and thanking them for their assistance he shared that he suffered occasionally with the "fits," which according to him, had been triggered this time around, by a "fresh cold" he was experiencing. As I got older, however, I gained a much better understanding of this thing called "fits"

In life we too experience "fits" of some sort as we go through our daily routines. Sometimes we are suddenly thrown down and overcome by unexpected challenges and circumstances. We cannot avoid these as we are told in 2 Timothy 3:12 that, "*All that will live godly in Christ Jesus shall suffer persecution.*" Despite this seemingly daunting prospect we are assured in Psalm 34:19 that, "*Many are the afflictions of the righteous but the Lord God delivers him out of them all.*" Knowing that, "*God is our refuge and strength, a very present help in trouble,"* (Psalm 46:1) is encouraging. In addition, in Proverbs 18:10 Solomon posits that, *"The name of the Lord is a strong tower: the righteous run into it and are safe."*

Just as that epileptic man was overcome by "fits" as Christians, we too face trials and tribulations. In the same way others came to his assistance, God offers us help in the form of His FITS - Favour in the Storm. In Isaiah 43:2 the Lord tells us,

> *"When you pass through the waters, I will be with you; and when you pass through the rivers, they will not sweep over you. When you walk through the fire, you will not be burned; the flames will not set you ablaze."*

With this type of reassurance I don't mind having God's FITS - Favour in the Storm - at all. After all He is Faithful in Tight Situations.

38

The Test

School! Studying! Teaching! Learning! And tests!

For many people just the thought of a test makes their palms sweaty, causes palpitations, makes them vomit, sends them to the toilet more frequently or gives rise to panic attacks. These kinds of responses are not isolated to weak students but those who do well will tell you they have experienced some of those same effects. Of course, when the results are back and they have passed there is a sigh of relief and the agony felt leading up to each test is soon quickly forgotten. In cases of failure there is a feeling of disappointment and dejection but if your desire to pass is great, corrections will need to follow and some relearning may need to take place before the test is taken again.

1 Corinthians 13 is referred to as the love chapter of the Bible. As I reread it prior to writing, I decided to take the test it offered. I asked myself:

1. Am I patient?
2. Am I kind?
3. Am I envious?
4. Do I boast?
5. Am I proud?
6. Do I dishonour others?
7. Am I selfish?
8. Am I easily angered?
9. Do I keep a record of wrongs?
10. Am I happy when bad befalls people?
11. Am I always happy to hear the truth?
12. Am I protective?
13. Do I always trust?
14. Am I always hopeful?

15. Do I persevere?
16. Do I fail?

As I critiqued myself I was ashamed. I had failed the test which caused me to conclude that I really am not "walking in love" as I should as I saw myself falling short in so many ways. However, before you are quick to condemn me, take the test yourself and honestly critique yourself. Did you answer "No" to at least 1 question? Then my friend, like me, you too, have failed. But don't beat up on yourself too much, which is what the devil would love us to do.

Remember, "*There is now no condemnation to them which are in Christ Jesus, who walk not after the flesh, but after the spirit.*" (Romans 8:1) Recognising one's shortcomings is the first step to dealing with them.

The next step is to make a conscious effort to rectify each one. Just as important as the test is, are the corrections which should follow.

1 John 4:7-12, and 16-18, clearly state,

> "*Beloved, let us love one another: for love is of God; and every one that loves is born of God, and knows God. [8]Whoever does not love does not know God; because God is love. [9]This is how God showed His love toward us: He sent His one and only Son into the world that we might live through him. [10]This is love: not that we loved God, but that He loved us and sent His Son as an atoning sacrifice for our sins. [11]Beloved, since God so loved us, we also ought to love one another. [12]No one has ever seen God; but if we love one another, God lives in us and His love is made complete in us. [16]God is love; and whoever lives in love lives in God and God in them. [17]This is how our love is made perfect, that we will have confidence on the day of judgment: because as He is, so are we in the world. [18]There is no fear in love; but perfect love drives out fear because fear has to do with punishment. The one who fears is not made perfect in love.*"

Finally, verse 21 tells us, *And He has given us this command: Anyone who loves God must also love their brother and sister.*"

The challenge is to . . .

Take the test but more importantly do the corrections!

39

Seconds, Anyone?

Like many people I have a few hobbies. Travelling and reading are but two, but what I really enjoy most are shopping and eating. You would think that for someone who likes to eat cooking would be on my things-I-like-to-do list. Well it's not. Anyone who knows my husband Lincoln and I would know that he is the cook and boy can he cook! For the past several years, every Sunday after church we would go out for lunch. Apart from the main course, my favourite part of any meal is the dessert. From childhood I have always loved pastries. It is no wonder therefore that when pastries are available and they are nice I find myself not doing a very good job of resisting having seconds and sometimes shamefully thirds. Since my husband is not a "desserts" person I would sometimes ask him to get another helping on my behalf. And of course he obliges.

He chooses to remind me of the error of my ways, however, whenever I complain about putting on weight and he enjoys imitating the obvious look of delight on my face each time I indulged in having seconds. I do acknowledge his chiding and will refrain for a while, albeit a short while, but it isn't long before I am back to having seconds.

Our God is also a God of seconds (and if I may add, thirds and fourths and fifths.). I hope you get the picture. He is patient and long-suffering and though we may fall several times whenever we go to Him and tell him we are truly sorry for what we have done, He stands willing and ready to forgive us.

Despite his failings the psalmist David, who was an adulterer and murderer, was also known as a man after God's own heart. "*After removing Saul He made David their king. God testified concerning him:*

I have found David son of Jesse, a man after my own heart; He will do everything I want him to do" Acts 13:22. Do you know what set David apart from others? He always expressed godly sorrow when he knew that he had done wrong. And God forgave him and gave him a second chance. The book of Psalms is to his credit.

In the book of Judges we also read about Samson, who was chosen by God and destined for greatness. However, he broke the vows he had made before God and found himself entangled with Delilah, a most unholy liaison. As a result, he was captured by his enemies, had his eyes gouged out and ridiculed. In Judges 16:28, however, we read how he cried out to God one more time and his prayer was answered. *"Sovereign Lord, remember me. Please, God, strengthen me just once more and let me with one blow get revenge on the Philistines for my two eyes."* In verse 30 he begged God to be allowed to die with the Philistines and God granted both his requests. Consequently, he avenged himself by killing more enemies in his death than in his entire life time. Though he had wandered away from God, when Samson repented and cried out to God He heard him and gave him a second chance.

Jesus' lineage can be traced back to the prostitute Rahab. Though a woman of dubious character her destiny was forever altered when she stepped out in faith and bravely hid the 12 Israelite men sent to spy out the Promised Land.

Like each of these 3 persons God has given us free will choice. It doesn't matter what we have done or how long we have been doing it, *"If we confess our sins, He is faithful and just and will forgive us our sins, and cleanse us from all unrighteousness"* (1 John 1:9). We will fall and sometimes hard too, but it's the staying down that impedes our progress. We need to get up and go again.

Years ago there was a song by a group called Shalamar which claimed, "Second time around is better than the first.[12]" Part of the song was:

---

[12] Song, *Second Time Around,* Shalamar, 2010

"You can't keep running away from love,
'Cause the first one let you down
And though others try to satisfy you, baby
With me true love can still be found."

While the artistes were not referring to God, the "me" in the lyrics could very well be referring to Him for with God we can find true love and the second time around is always so much better than the first. We may try other things - people, cars, alcohol, drugs, fame, fortune, etc. True satisfaction, however, can only be found in Jesus. Acts 4:12 is clear, "*Neither is there salvation in any other: for there is no other name under heaven, given among men, whereby we must be saved.*" That name is Jesus and because God is faithful our future with Him is so much brighter.

Another songwriter posits:

"Faithful, faithful, faithful is our God
And I rejoice today for I shall recover it all!"[13]

Nothing is lost with God. Rather there is everything to gain. "*For what shall it profit a man if he should gain the whole world and lose his own soul*" (Matthew 16:26).

Don't take chances!

Seconds anyone?

---

[13] Song *Faithful, Faithful, Faithful is our God*, Hezekiah Walker, 2008

40

Y or N

Holders of UK passports are privileged in that they need not obtain a US visa in order to travel to the US. They can instead get a visa waiver, obtained by applying for an "ESTA" (Electronic System for Travel Authorization).

Many years ago, I successfully applied for a 10 year visa on behalf of my son who was still a student at the time and who was in possession of a Barbados passport. However, after leaving school and following the expiration of the visa he reapplied for a new one but was denied. By virtue of me being a UK citizen he too was entitled to a UK passport and so he decided to apply for one. After obtaining it, he decided to travel to Miami.

Just like with the visa application before, he had to complete a form consisting of a series of key Y/N (Yes/No) questions, one of which was, "Have you ever been denied a US visa?" Should you answer Y to any of these questions you are advised to visit the US embassy closest to you before travelling to the States. Since his obvious answer to this question was "Yes" then it meant that this was his next step. When he first contacted the consulate he was told by one employee that as a holder of a UK passport he did not need a visa but he pointed out to them (as if that should have been necessary) that he had previously been denied a visa and was following the instructions on the application. Long story short, my son now has the distinction of having a UK passport complete with a US visa!

In life we have one key Y/N question, the answer to which will have favourable or dire consequences for each of us.

That question is: Do you accept Jesus as your personal Lord and Saviour?

Just as it is necessary for non-US citizens to apply for a visa to enter the US, if we want to enter the kingdom of God we need to make application because we are told in Romans 3:23 that, "*All have sinned and come short of the glory of God.*" Because we cannot enter God's kingdom in our sinful state we need to accept the offer extended to everyone by Jesus.

In Revelation 3:20, He says, "*Here I am! I stand at the door and knock: If anyone hears my voice and opens the door, I will come in and eat with that person, and they with me.*" Depending on the response to the invitation the "visa" can either be granted or denied. Interestingly enough, the possession of a US visa does not guarantee you entry at any US port, which is ultimately left to the discretion of the border control officers. Conversely though, when Christ issues His "visa", entry to God's kingdom IS GUARANTEED.

The rewards and consequences for how we answer the question, "Do you accept Jesus as your personal Lord and Saviour?" are stated clearly in Romans 6:23, "*For the wages of sin is death; but the gift of God is eternal life through Jesus Christ our Lord.*"

A "Yes" response to the invitation will result in hearing the words from Matthew 25:23, "*Well done, good and faithful servant; . . . enter thou into the joy of the Lord.*" A "No" answer on the other hand will generate the dreaded words from Matthew 25:41, "*Then He will say to those on his left, "Depart from me, you who are cursed, into the eternal fire prepared for the devil and his angels.*" At that point there are no second chances or waivers.

So what will your answer be? Y or N?

41

Of Audits and Auditors![14]

I was talking to a friend recently and she was lamenting the fact that external auditors were currently visiting her place of employment. As a senior employee, she was working closely with them as they sought to conduct an unbiased and official financial examination of the top organization's accounts. While it is critically important for any business to accurately account for all income and expenditure it was so frustrating for her that she vowed that this would definitely be her last time as she was not prepared to go through another one.

According to her, each time information was requested and provided the auditors were seemingly dissatisfied and wanted more. This wouldn't have been so bad if it was a matter of one or two pages but in many cases each additional request involved reports several pages long! As a result each work day was much longer than usual as both she and the auditors would arrive early in the morning and work very late into the night. It was obviously a very tiring exercise. Despite the long hours, the intensity, the frustrations and the frayed nerves as a result of any audit, every company looks forward to and welcomes having a "qualified" report at the end of it all. This is viewed as a "fair representation of the position of the company without any material misrepresentation."

On the other hand whenever the investigations unearth inaccuracies, suggesting that it is not a fair representation, then the auditors' report is deemed "unqualified" and issues for action are highlighted and recommendations - some of which are not

---

[14] *Wikipedia Internet Reference* accessed 26th *July 2015*

always welcomed - are made quite clear. My friend, her fellow employees and her employers will, no doubt, be thrilled to receive a favourable report.

There is coming a day when each of us will also have to stand before the master auditor, God, and we too will be audited. Sadly many persons believe that when we depart from this life that that is the end. However, the word of God tells us in Hebrews 9:27 that, *"It is appointed unto men once to die, but after this the judgment."* This means that we will all have to stand before God, the righteous judge, to give an account of what we have done in our lifetime and nothing will be hidden.

> *"And I saw the dead, small and great, stand before God; and the books were opened: and another book was opened, which is the book of life: and the dead were judged out of those things which were written in the books, according to their works"* (Revelation 20:12).

> *"For there is nothing covered that will not be revealed, and hidden that will not be known"* (Matthew 10:26).

And ALL deeds, whether good or bad will be rewarded. Jesus tells us in Revelation 22:12, *"And, behold, I come quickly; and my reward is with me, to give every man according as his work shall be."*

Let us pause for a moment and ask ourselves, What kind of report will I receive from THE auditor?

Will it be qualified or unqualified, favourable or unfavourable?

A favourable report will receive a commendation from God. The reward? Eternal life with Him.

> *"And I heard a great voice out of heaven saying, Behold, the tabernacle of God is with men, and He will dwell with them, and they shall be His people, and God himself shall be with them, and be their God"* (Revelation 21:3).

An unfavourable one will result in the most serious of irreversible recommendations. *"And whosoever was not found written in the book of life was cast into the lake of fire"* (Revelation 20:15).

During the final audit there won't be any more opportunities to make any adjustments or rectify any wrongs but we can use the time NOW to properly prepare ourselves for that inevitable final audit!

42

Blinkers[15] Anyone?

If you have ever watched or followed horse racing you would have noticed that many race horses wear a contraption around their eyes called blinkers. These blinkers or blinders as they are sometimes called are a piece of horse tack that prevents the horse from seeing to the rear and in some cases, to the side. According to horse enthusiasts "field shy" horses and those that run about while racing, improve dramatically when blinkers are added. This piece of equipment can actually help horses to settle down as it causes them to shut out the busyness around them. Now in "switched on" mode they are now able to focus on the race course but more importantly the finish line, hoping of course to be first past the post.

After horses have grown accustomed to blinkers owners can actually remove them with positive effect. For many thoroughbred trainers, dramatic shifts in form can be attributed to the application of blinkers, which they regard as a critical tool and which, when used wisely, will help them and their "charges" to win races. The rewards for winning are varied - ribbons, lucrative financial gains, cups and finally being dubbed the champion horse, while being paraded around for all to see.

As we go through life we sometimes find ourselves off track and it is necessary to refocus. In Matthew 7:13-14 we are told,

> *"Enter through the narrow gate. For wide is the gate and broad is the road that leads to destruction, and many enter through it. But small is the gate and narrow the road that leads to life, and only a few find it."*

---

[15] *Wikipedia Internet Reference* accessed 28th July 2015

Jesus warns us in Luke 13:24 to *"Make every effort to enter through the narrow door, because many, will try to enter and will not be able to."* Life is replete with seemingly attractive distractions - alcohol, drugs, sex, TV, partying, our jobs, hobbies, family - which we sometimes unwittingly allow to consume us at the expense of spending quality time with God and developing a meaningful relationship with Him. Satan deceives us into thinking that we are on the right track and that is why the Bible says in 2 Corinthians 4:4 that, *"The god of this age has blinded the minds of unbelievers so that they cannot see the light of the gospel that displays the glory of Christ."*

We need therefore to follow the advice of 1 Thessalonians 5:22, and *"Shun the very appearance of evil,"* and James 4:7, *"Submit yourselves to God. Resist the devil and he will flee from you."* That's why we too need spiritual blinkers so that we will not lose sight of our ultimate goal. When Joshua took over the mantle from Moses he was cautioned, *"Be careful to obey all the law...do not turn from it to the right or to the left, that you may be successful wherever you go"* (Joshua 1:7).

Our aim is to read and obey God's word in order to keep our focus as we head to the finish line so that on successful completion of the course we would be able to declare like the apostle Paul,

> *"I have fought the good fight, I have finished the race, I have kept the faith. Now there is in store for me the crown of righteousness, which the Lord, the righteous judge, will award to me on that day"* (2 Timothy 4:7-8).

Blinkers anyone?

43

Hide and Seek

Once upon a time "Hide and Seek" was one of the most popular games that children enjoyed playing. This was of course before TV, computers, cell phones, video games, play stations, X-boxes and tablets (not the eating kind) came along.

In the game, one person would cover their eyes and count at least to ten, while the other person or persons would scamper away to find a safe and secure place to hide. When the counter was ready he or she would shout, "Ready or not, here I come!" and they would set out to try to find the hiding place(s) of each one. More often than not each person was discovered but occasionally one or two were so well hidden that they had to reveal themselves. Though just a game it really did stir up the creative juices in the players.

Although the instances of kids playing the game these days seem to be getting rarer and rarer the concept of HIDE and SEEK has been around since time immemorial and there are several references to it in the Bible.

HIDE

"Keep me as the apple of the eye, HIDE me under the shadow of thy wings." Psalm 17:8

"For in the time of trouble He shall HIDE me in His pavilion: in the secret of His tabernacle shall He HIDE me." Psalm 27:5

"HIDE thy face from my sins, and blot out all mine iniquities," Psalm 51:9

"Deliver me, O Lord, from mine enemies: I flee unto thee to HIDE. Psalm 143:9

"Can any HIDE himself in secret places that I shall not see him? saith the Lord." Jeremiah 23:24

SEEK

"For the Son of man is come to SEEK and to save that which was lost." Luke 19:10

"I will SEEK that which was lost, and bring again that which was driven away." Ezekiel 34: 16

"SEEK the Lord while He may be found; call on Him while He is near." Isaiah 55:6

"Now set your heart and your soul to SEEK the Lord your God." 1 Chronicles 22:19

"That they should SEEK the Lord, if haply they might reach out for Him and find Him, though He be not far from every one of us." Acts 17:27

"It is time to SEEK the Lord." Hosea 10:12

"But SEEK ye first the kingdom of God and His righteousness, and all other things shall be added unto you." Matthew 6:33

"If you SEEK Him, He will be found by you, but if you forsake Him He will reject you forever." 1 Chronicles 28:9

These are but just some of the verses showing us that God has long been in the business of HIDE and SEEK. Against all odds, Holocaust survivor Corrie Ten Boom managed to escape the fate that nearly 6 million Jews suffered. Throughout her ordeal she was able to hide herself in God for there is where she found complete solace. Her book "The Hiding Place[16]" is testament to that. Jesus came to provide a place of hiding for us where we will always be safe and secure. We need to SEEK Him out and HIDE in that place of abode.

Want to play HIDE and SEEK?

---

[16] *The Hiding Place,* Corrie Ten Boom, 1971

44
Heads/Tails

Whether it is the start of a team sport or it's an individual competition some games afford competitors or the captain of the team the opportunity to make an initial choice, either for service (tennis), centre pass or shooting area (netball), kickoff (football), batting or fielding (cricket or baseball), playing first (darts, pool) or simply a direction - North/South, East/West, prior to the start of a match. The determination will usually be made by the flick of a coin.

As the coin is tossed into the air one of the decision makers will call "Heads" or "Tails". Sometimes the coin is caught in midair and slapped onto the back of the tosser's hand. Whichever way is chosen the winner is the person whose side of the coin is facing upwards at the end of it all and he or she then signals their intention to the other party leaving them with the other available option whether they wanted it or not.

For many competitors winning the toss gives them a psychological advantage over their opponent(s) as for them it's the ideal way to start any match. As a sporting enthusiast I have discovered that when taking a toss the majority of people shout, "Heads". They might not all win but it seems to be the preferred option. There seems to be something significant and powerful about the "Head." Have you ever noticed that though all different parts of a body may be transplanted a "head" never is? While all the parts of the body are important, in my estimation the head is even more so since we would cease to exist without one. God in His infinite wisdom designed us exactly like this and that is why the psalmist says in Psalm 139:14, "*I will praise thee; for I am fearfully and wonderfully made.*" In corporations though different persons are tasked with varying responsibilities, it is the CEO (Chief Executive Officer) or Head of the organisation who is ultimately responsible for making managerial decisions whether they are related to hiring, firing or payment of salaries.

If we obey God's word we are told in Deuteronomy 28:13 that,

> *"The Lord shall make you the head and not the tail; and you shall be above only, and you shall not be beneath; if you pay attention to the commands of the Lord your God, which I give you this day, to observe and to do them."*

Forget about the tail and determine to work towards being a head with a bright future. Declare today that you are the Head and not the tail.

45

Sitting On The Fence

I was recently watching a video with my students about Running of the Bulls[17] in Spain. Ever year in the month of July there is a festival in San Fermin which is characterized by people being chased through narrow streets by a set of bulls, with the chase ending in La Plaza de Toros (the Bull ring). Despite the possibility of injury this well-loved sport forms an integral part of Spanish culture. Along the route many persons view the activity from balconied buildings while some also stand behind or sit on barricades or fences to view the proceedings. What was amazing in this particular video were the instances of persons perched on fences, who were charged by a bull.

As they watched the goings-on from their supposedly safe vantage points these persons were oblivious to the danger which was lurking. Many were caught unaware as the bull rushed toward them. Those who were swift enough to take evasive action hurriedly jumped off the fence, while the not-so-fortunate ones toppled backwards, suffering injury in the process.

As I watched those persons sitting on the fence it brought to mind Matthew 6:24 which says, "*No man can serve two masters: for either he will hate the one, and love the other; or else he will hold to the one, and despise the other. You cannot serve God and mammon.*"

Here it is these people opted not to take part in the running but still wanted a piece of the action, from a place which seemed safe to them -a fence- which turned out to be not that safe after all. When it comes to making a decision for Christ we must make our position clear. We

---

[17] *Running of the Bulls* Pamplona Spain, *June 2007*

are either for Him or we are against Him. There is no middle ground and sitting on the fence can be detrimental to your eternal future.

We need therefore to *"Choose this day whom you will serve…As for me and my house, we will serve the Lord"* Joshua 24:15.

Be careful sitting on the fence.

46

Excess Baggage

I am currently writing this on an airplane and shortly after takeoff there was the usual announcement informing passengers about the safety features and what should be done in the case of an emergency.

As a frequent traveler I am very aware of these announcements. What really struck me this time around however was the stipulation which said, "In the case of an evacuation please leave all hand luggage behind, I immediately started some serious introspection and chided myself for flouting the same instruction during the fire drills at school.

Each time there is one I always grab my handbag before exiting the building. It really made me think, and I was reminded of Lot's wife who was turned into a pillar of salt because she "looked back." Instead of focusing on getting out of Sodom and Gomorrah with her life intact she kept thinking about what she would be leaving behind. Why would anyone choose to grab their handbag in an emergency? The answer: To secure the earthly possessions deemed valuable, which will, ironically, fade away with time. The Bible warns us in Matthew 6:19-21, "*Lay not up for yourselves treasures upon earth. . . But lay up for yourselves treasures in heaven. For where your treasure is, there will your heart be also.*"

Jesus is very clear in Luke 9:24, "*For whosoever will save his life shall lose it: but whosoever will lose his life for my sake the same shall save it.*" Anyone, yours truly included, who would think about grabbing their bag in the midst of potential disaster instead of fleeing for his/her life has his/her priorities in the wrong place And you know what? God has more than enough resources to replace whatever may be in that bag, anyway.

Philippians 4:19 emphasizes this, "*But my God shall supply all your need according to His riches in glory by Christ Jesus.*" This episode is a timely reminder that there is nothing more important than eternal life and to secure it we need to rid ourselves of excess baggage which will only weigh us down and could be the deciding factor between our eternal life and death. Besides, when we give up or lose something for Jesus, the returns are always phenomenal.

> "*And Jesus answered and said, Verily I say unto you, There is no man that hath left house, or brethren, or sisters, or father, or mother, or wife, or children, or lands, for my sake, and the gospel's, But he shall receive an hundredfold now in this time, houses, and brethren, and sisters, and mothers, and children, and lands, with persecutions; and in the world to come eternal life.*" Mark 10:29-30

So get rid of the excess baggage. It isn't worth losing your life over it.

47

Cul-de-sac

Have you ever driven down a road thinking that you were on the right track to reach your destination, only to discover that it was a dead-end? Well it has happened to me several times and each time I have to reverse, turn around and find the correct route. People who know me well will tell you that I usually refer to myself as being "directionally-challenged". It doesn't matter how many times I've visited some places I have great difficulty finding them again and again. Thank God I have an excellent navigator for a husband!

I remember when she was only four years of age, my granddaughter directed me, the chauffeur, to the apartment where her parents lived! I've reached the point where I simply acknowledge this as a shortcoming and make no apologies for it. Perhaps that is because there is usually someone else there to rely on; in most cases it's my husband. Whenever directions are involved I would just hand the phone over to him, much to his chagrin at times. I have not been able to convince him, however, that my brain just doesn't seem to process directions like his does. As it is right now I appear to be at a dead-end in that area of my life. Some would argue that I am a prime candidate to receive the book "Directions for Dummies." But I guess if I really wanted and needed to and with greater effort and reliance on God, I could make an improvement. Philippians 4:13 cannot be clearer when it says, *"I can do all things through Christ who strengthens me."*

There are other more important things in our life where we too find ourselves in a cul-de-sac. We pray for the fruit of the spirit of Galatians 5:22 - love, joy, peace, longsuffering (patience), gentleness, goodness, faithfulness, kindness and self-control - and we are able to quote Philippians 4:8,

"Finally, brethren, whatsoever things are true, whatsoever things are honest, whatsoever things are just, whatsoever things are pure, whatsoever things are lovely, whatsoever things are of good report; if there be any virtue, and if there be any praise, think on these things,"

But whenever we find ourselves in situations where we need to exhibit these qualities and characteristics it seems as if we, too, have reached a cul-de-sac.

Though not always easy, we don't have to stay in those dead-ends of our life. We can recalibrate and get back on track. We can be guided by Romans 12:2, *"And be not conformed to this world: but be ye transformed by the renewing of your mind, that you may prove what is that good, and acceptable, and perfect, will of God."* As we submit to God and yield to His leading, we can be victorious over those areas in our lives which challenge us the most.

Are you in a cul-de-sac? Then recalibrate.

48

Carnival Time

Many countries in the Caribbean and throughout the world have some sort of national celebration with a carnival-like atmosphere. There is Trinidad and Tobago carnival, Vincy mas (St. Vincent), Spice mas (Grenada), Grand Kadooment (Barbados), Jamaica Carnival, Notting Hill Carnival (U. K.) Labour Day weekend (U.S.), Quebec Winter Carnival (Canada) and the very popular Brazilian Carnival.

According to Sessions Magazine[18], "Carnival is an annual CHRISTIAN festival." Truth be told, however, if you were to witness the behaviour and dress of many of the revellers you would deduce that it is more devilish than Godly. Many of these festivals, however, indeed started out as celebrations about God's goodness, but many have degenerated into a grand old party, punctuated with lewd, crude, bad behaviour, compliments of our age old enemy, the devil, who would do anything in his power to tarnish what was originally created for God's glory. We could, though, learn a lot from some of these people who jump and wave and gyrate and are merry with gay abandon.

We could learn how to show our gratitude with some of their attitude. When we consider what God has done for us, we ought to praise Him like there is no tomorrow. In 2 Samuel 6:14 we are told, *"And David danced before the Lord with all his might;"* until his clothes fell off. (Verse 20). I am not advocating, that we go around naked or half naked, of course, or that we indulge in the shameful behaviour of some revellers, but our praise should be such that we work up a good sweat just like those revellers do and just like David did. We have much to jump and wave and clap and dance and shout about. Psalm

---

[18] Sessions Magazine Internet Reference accessed 4th August 2015

126:3 tells us, "*The Lord has done great things for us, whereof we are glad.*" And you know what? We don't deserve any of it, but it is because of God's mercies that we can truly enjoy His goodness.

One songwriter says:

> *We're blest, we're blest, we're blest, We are blest,*
> *Shelter, clothing and strength, we are blessed . . .*
> *We don't deserve it but yet we are blessed[19]."*

Therefore we ought to, "*Give thanks unto the Lord, for He is good: for His mercy endures forever*" Psalm 107:1. Remember, even in the bad times God is still good and despite what you may be going through someone else somewhere is experiencing something worse.

Every day should be treated like the way carnivals were created to be, celebrations of God's goodness. So, give thanks with a grateful heart and let's show God gratitude with attitude.

---

[19] Song *We're Blest*, Nazarene Silvertones, Internet Reference accessed 4th August 2015

49

Don't Worry! Be Happy!

I remember when Bobby McFerrin released the song, "Don't Worry, Be Happy[20]" in 1988, it was an instant hit and many of the lyrics are still applicable today.

The most poignant parts of the song for me state:

In every life we have some trouble
When you worry you make it double
So don't worry, be happy.
'Cause when you worry your face will frown
And that will bring everybody down.
So don't worry, be happy."

Has that been your experience too? It sure has been mine. Here's something a friend sent to me the day before I wrote this. Not sure if it's true or not but it offers another perspective on worrying:

"The great comedian Charlie Chaplin[21] once told an audience a wonderful joke and all the people started laughing...

Chaplin repeated the same joke and only a few people laughed... He again repeated the same joke but this time no one laughed..."

This was his response: "You cannot laugh at the same joke again and again...then why do you cry again and again on the same worry?" Interesting, isn't it? Why worry about the same worry, which doesn't seem to be changing. Chaplin's adage was to enjoy every moment of

---

[20] *Don't Worry Be Happy* Bobby McFerrin, *1988*
[21] *Whataspp Reference 5th August 2015*

life because it is beautiful. Here are three statements which have been attributed to him:

1. There is nothing permanent in this world, not even our troubles.
2. I like walking in the rain, because nobody can see my tears.
3. The most wasted day in life is the day in which we have not laughed.

Sounds very philosophical and there is some merit in the words, but hear the words of Jesus in Matthew 11:28-30,

> *"Come unto me, all you that labour and are heavy laden, and I will give you rest. Take my yoke upon you, and learn of me; for I am meek and lowly in heart: and you shall find rest to your souls. For my yoke is easy and my burden is light."*

Carrying around the worries on our own will make us look glum and gloomy and will only weigh us down and that's why Jesus said to offload them on Him. Plus, it takes more energy to frown than it does to smile.

So, don't worry, be happy; and keep smiling. 😁 😁 😁

50

It's SOY Time

Many years ago soy was regarded as a miracle health food with its use rapidly gaining in popularity. Nutritionists were touting its greatness and where choices were available soy products got the nod with soy milk being one of those choices. Fast forward a few years and we start to hear about the dangers of the same product, causing persons to look for other replacements. The jury is still undecided, however, on the dangers of soy, and soy sauce, used to enhance the taste of many dishes, is still quite popular in several restaurants.

In the Cayman Islands there is a foundation known as the SOY foundation. This however has nothing to do with the popular legume but is an organization set up to Save Our Youth. No one would disagree that babies and young children are the apples of our eye and everyone delights in them. However, as they get older so too do the concerns about them begin to grow. Many an adult has been heard to lament, "They don't listen." "They don't go to church." "They are lazy." "They are so untidy." And the rants go on. Our children are changing at a rapid rate and not all the change is to our liking. Isn't it remarkable how we only seem to notice the change AFTER it takes place and hardly ever WHILE it's happening?

Psalm 127:3 tells us that, "*Children are a heritage (gift) from the Lord, and the fruit of the womb is his reward.*" In the same way as we would treasure a gift received and would expect people to take care of one given to them by us, we should treat children in like fashion. Given to us by God, we ALL have a collective responsibility to take care of them as it really does take a village to raise a child.

In the corporate world people who are solution-focused are paid more attention than those who simply complain. Sure, there may be problems but bosses are more interested in knowing what is your answer for solving the issue. With our children we need to get back to the basics:

1. Teach them about God. This is the tech age and there are free interactive Bible apps for kids. Download them onto their tablets and spend time going through the stories with them.

2. We should follow Jesus' advice in Matthew 19:14 when He says, "*Let the little children come to me, and do not hinder them, for the kingdom of heaven belongs to such as these.*" Send them to Sunday school AND let them accompany you to church. We don't let them decide if they go to school or not so why not take the same militant approach to the things of God. "*The kingdom of heaven suffers violence and the violent take it by force.*" Matthew 11:12

3. Pray for and with them and encourage them to do likewise. Praying before meals is a good starting point.

4. Demonstrate good Christian character as much as possible (especially when they get you upset.) and be consistent.

5. Know their friends. "*Bad company corrupts good character.*" 1 Corinthians 15:33

6. Speak positively about them, encourage them and make declarations over their life: "*You are fearfully and wonderfully made.*" Psalm 139:14 "*You are the head and not the tail, above and not beneath.*" Deuteronomy 28:13. "*You can do all things through Christ who gives you strength.*" Philippians 4:13

We keep hearing that the young people today are destined to be the leaders of tomorrow, so if we want godly leaders in the future we need to start shaping and moulding them now.

> *Train up a child in the way he (or she) should go and when he (or she) is old he (or she) will not depart from it.*" Proverbs 22:6

There is no doubt about it. There is a battle raging and the children of the world are the targets. It is SOY -Save Our Youth - time.

Any volunteers?

51

Have You Acquired The Taste?

There are some foods that I think you simply have to acquire the taste for and for me an olive is one such food. I remember the first time I encountered this vegetable, I was on a British Airways flight to England. I actually thought they were grapes and since I love grapes I relished eating them until I took the first bite. Ugh. I spat it out in a hurry.

In later years, I discovered that this "awful" tasting food item was an olive! Though not having the most pleasant of tastes, according to health experts olives offer a host of benefits. They are rich in iron, vitamin E and copper, are an excellent source of fibre and contain monosaturated fats which reduce the risk of atherosclerosis and increase HDL (good) cholesterol. For me, eating an olive reminds me of the Buckley's cough syrup advertisement which says, "It tastes awful but it works." Kudos to my husband who has already acquired the taste for them. Though I struggle to eat them I have no hesitation however in using olive oil and many olive-oil related products. But the process whereby olive oil is made is intense.

The olives have to be shaken, beaten and pressed in order to extract the oil which is a precious commodity. As God's creation we too will go through periods of shaking, beating and pressing before our precious oil comes forth. These times might not be palatable but they will be for our good.

Hebrews 12:5-11 says,

> "My son, do not make light of the Lord's discipline, and do not
> lose heart when He rebukes you, ⁶Because the Lord disciplines
> the one He loves, and He chastens everyone he accepts as His

son. ⁷If you endure chastening, God is dealing with you as his children. For what children are not disciplined by their father? ⁸If you are not chastened — and everyone undergoes discipline — then you are not legitimate, not true sons and daughters at all. ⁹Moreover, we have all had human fathers who disciplined us and we respected them for it. How much more should we submit to the Father of spirits and live? ¹⁰They chastened us for a little while as they thought best; but God disciplines us for our good, in order that we may share in His holiness. ¹¹No discipline seems pleasant at the time, but painful. Later on, however, it produces a harvest of righteousness and peace for those who have been trained by it."

As we go through our shaking and beating and pressing, it may not "taste" good but the benefits are tremendous.

Have you acquired the taste yet? It's time.

52

All For One and One For All!

If you have ever watched the movie or read the book then you know that the title is a quote from The Three Musketeers[22]. It came to mind as I was ending a cruise when I saw the cruise motto, "All for fun and fun for all." If you want to know what it means for someone to have your back check out the three musketeers. Each one is committed to the group and when they go into battle that is their battle cry, "All for one and one for all." No matter the number of opponents being faced the musketeers believe that the odds are stacked in their favour when they present themselves as a united force.

There is certainly no fun attached to it at all like the cruise liner says. Instead these men mean serious business. Wouldn't it be great if Christians worldwide adopted that type of attitude? If we all presented a united front against our arch enemy, the devil, mountains would come tumbling down at an alarming rate. It is to be noted that in Acts 2:1 the disciples were, "*All with one accord,*" prior to being empowered by the Holy Spirit. If we want to see the power of God like never before then we need to be united. Romans 12:5 tells us that, "*We, being many, are one body in Christ, and every one members one of another.*"

We are also advised in verse 10 to, "*Be kindly affectioned one to another with brotherly love; in honour preferring one another* and in verse 15 to, "*Rejoice with them that do rejoice, and weep with then that weep.*" When Jesus gave His life it was One for All. We now need to fulfill our end of the bargain as we live, All for One, and dedicate our lives to complete service to Him in thanksgiving for His ultimate sacrifice.

---

[22] *The Three Musketeers,* Alexandre Dumas 1993

In Acts 10:34 and 35 we are told that, "*God is no respecter of persons. But in every nation he that feareth Him and worketh righteousness, is accepted with Him,*" For, "*He is Lord of all*" (Verse 36).

We are His and He is ours so let the battle cry resound, "All for one and one for all.

53

In The Nick Of Time

These days, unlike years gone by my husband and I usually make a list of stuff we need prior to travelling. One of the items on our list during one of our recent holidays was a large umbrella. We knew what we wanted but it wasn't until our final day on our way to the airport that we stopped and purchased it. Once at the airport we checked our bags, got the all clear to carry the umbrella with us, went through security and proceeded to the gate. We were quite early so while I sat and played a game my husband went off walking.

About two hours later we were sitting in our seats on the airplane and then he asked, "Where is the umbrella?" It was then we realized that we, or rather he, had left it behind somewhere. As we sat pondering where he might have left it (my thinking was that he might dash off to get it before take-off) and lamenting (that was me) that after all that trouble and some expense we had left the umbrella somewhere, my husband nonchalantly said, "That's life. It just wasn't meant to be!" Would you believe that as soon as he had said it down walks the flight attendant carrying two umbrellas in her hands and one of them was ours! She was seeking out the owners just minutes before the aircraft door closed. Whew, just in the nick of time! My only comment after thanking her profusely was, "God is so amazing. We were just talking about losing the umbrella and you turn up with the umbrella." Now how awesome is that!

In John 11:1-44, when Jesus' friend Lazarus took ill, his sisters Mary and Martha sent word to Jesus, but instead of departing right away to visit Lazarus, Jesus responds in verse 4 by saying, "*This sickness will not end in death. No, it is for God's glory, so that God's Son may be glorified through it.*" He opts to stay on for two more days. When Jesus finally arrives, Lazarus is dead and has been for 4 days! This doesn't deter Jesus, however, as He commands Lazarus in verse 43 to come forth and Lazarus does! We are reminded by Jesus in verse 25 that He is, *"The resurrection and the life."*

In life we will have disappointments. Our dreams may seem shattered, loved ones will disappoint, our health or businesses may be going downhill, job prospects may look dim, financial woes may beset us and the litany of problems may go on, but don't lose heart, Jesus will always show up in the nick of time to bring new life to seemingly dead situations.

Remember a delay doesn't mean a denial. It is just an opportunity for God to show up and show off. He always delivers, just in the nick of time, for us, but right on time for Him.

54

I Dare You

Many children and adults too, can be heard saying to others, "I dare you," or even, "I double dare you." The words are meant to spur on another person to complete some type of challenge.

Challenges may be as simple as taking fruit from a tree, chatting up someone of the opposite sex or staying overnight in a haunted house to something more difficult such as smoking a cigarette, drinking alcohol, taking drugs, beating up someone, sleeping with someone, stealing stuff or participating in a drive-by shooting, all of which can have serious life-changing consequences. Regardless to the challenge, however, the person who takes it up does so to "prove" something to the one issuing the dare. They want to show that they are capable and "powerful". By doing so successfully they often earn the respect of the challenger and depending on the level of danger faced, sometimes they are feared by them as well.

Daring or testing is not a new concept however as it is seen in the book of Exodus. In chapter 2:23-25 the enslaved Israelites tested God as they cried out to Him for deliverance.

> *The Israelites groaned in their slavery and cried out, and their cry for help because of their slavery went up to God. God heard their groaning and He remembered His covenant with Abraham, with Isaac and with Jacob. So God looked on the Israelites and was concerned about them."*

God promised to deliver them from the hand of their Egyptian oppressors. In verses 7 and 8 of chapter 3 He said,

"I have indeed seen the misery of my people in Egypt. I have heard them crying out because of their slave drivers and I am concerned about their suffering. So I have come down to rescue them from the hand of the Egyptians and to bring them up out of that land into a good and spacious land, a land flowing with milk and honey."

They put God to the test, He took up the challenge and He succeeded. However instead of gaining greater respect His ability was challenged. He was dared and even double-dared every step of the way.

In Exodus 5:22-23, even Moses, God's chosen leader for the deliverance, questioned God's ability,

"Moses returned to the Lord and said, "Why, Lord, why have you brought trouble on this people? Is this why you sent me? Ever since I went to Pharaoh to speak in your name, he has brought trouble on this people, and you have not rescued your people at all."

God responds in chapter 6:1-3, 6-8, by saying,

"Now you will see what I will do to Pharaoh: Because of my mighty hand he will let them go; because of my mighty hand he will drive them out of his country. God also said to Moses, "I am the Lord. I appeared to Abraham, to Isaac and to Jacob as God Almighty, but by my name the Lord I did not make myself fully known to them. . .Therefore, say to the Israelites: 'I am the Lord , and I will bring you out from under the yoke of the Egyptians. I will free you from being slaves to them, and I will redeem you with an outstretched arm and with mighty acts of judgment. I will take you as my own people, and I will be your God. Then you will know that I am the Lord your God, who brought you out from under the yoke of the Egyptians. And I will bring you to the land I swore with uplifted hand to give to Abraham, to Isaac and to Jacob. I will give it to you as a possession. I am the Lord.' "

God had made a promise and He had a foolproof plan but the Israelites just couldn't help complaining. In Exodus 15, they complained about having bitter water and He made it sweet. Again in chapter 16 they complained about not having food and God sent bread for them to eat. As if that wasn't enough they murmured about too much bread and so God gave them quail (meat). In chapter 17 they dared Him to get them water and again He achieved the feat. And when they were threatened by the Amalekites God secured victory for them.

Amazing though that despite successfully completing every challenge and proving Himself, the children of Israel still were not satisfied. And to think that for the 40 years of wandering they didn't need a change of clothes or footwear. Now how cool is that! They even went as far as accusing God of not being able to deliver them! As a matter of fact they were the ones who failed the test issued to them by God! *"Then the Lord said to Moses, "I will rain down bread from heaven for you. The people are to go out each day and gather enough for that day. In this way I will test them and see whether they will follow my instructions"* (Exodus 16: 4).

> *"Moses said to the people, "Do not be afraid. God has come to test you, so that the fear of God will be with you to keep you from sinning"* (Exodus 20:20). (See also Deuteronomy 8:2 and 16.)

Before we start being so critical of the children of Israel though let us thoroughly examine ourselves. God's goodness, love and mercy are extended to each of us daily yet we complain constantly. He doesn't have to do it but He does and all He requires from us is obedience. When we complain we are underestimating and questioning God's ability to do what He says He can and will do.

In Malachi 3:8-12 He dares us to prove Him now.

> *"Will a mere mortal rob God? Yet you rob me. "But you ask, 'How are we robbing you?' "In tithes and offerings. [9]You are under a curse – your whole nation – because you are robbing me. [10]Bring the whole tithe into the storehouse, that there may be food in my house. Test me in this," says the Lord Almighty, "and see if I will not throw open the floodgates of heaven and pour out so*

much blessing that there will not be room enough to store it. [11]I will prevent pests from devouring your crops, and the vines in your fields will not drop their fruit before it is ripe," says the Lord Almighty. "[12]Then all the nations will call you blessed, for yours will be a delightful land," says the Lord Almighty."

I Dare You: Dare God! Put Him to the test and see not whether He will deliver or not, but how He will deliver. Remember He is the same God now as He was back then and if He has done it before He can and will do it again.

55

Let Go AND Hold On

What a strange title as these two concepts seem so diametrically opposed to each other. You are probably thinking it's an error and should be Let Go OR Hold on for one cannot possibly let go and hold on at the same time. Actually there is no error as it is all about the context. I was watching part of the movie Gravity[23] recently and in the end when the last surviving astronaut found herself in the ocean in a capsule which was fast filling with water, she tried desperately to swim to the surface but struggled because her space suit was simply way too heavy. She had to first free herself of it in order to be able to swim to the surface of the water. That was the only way out as she held on tightly to her only hope of survival.

In our daily life, we too need to Let Go of those things that weigh us down, which will hinder us from dwelling sweetly and safely in God's presence. Hebrews 12:1 tells us, *"Let us lay aside every weight, and the sin which so easily besets us,"* and Romans 12:9 states, *"Abhor (Hate) that which is evil."*

Proverbs 6: 16-19 identify 7 such weights,

> *"There are six things the Lord hates, seven that are detestable to Him: haughty eyes, a lying tongue, hands that shed innocent blood, a heart that devises wicked schemes, feet that are quick to rush to evil, a false witness who pours out lies and a person who stirs up conflict in the community."*

---

[23] *Gravity* Alfonso Cuarón 2013

But perhaps we could also add envy, jealousy, unforgiveness, bitterness, being easily offended, hatred, gossip and materialism! You might even be able to think of some more things which hinder our walk with God.

As we release those types of weights we need to Hold On, but Hold on to what, you may ask? The second half of Romans 12:9 commands us to, *"Cling to what is good."*

And again in Philippians 4:8 we are told: *"Finally, brothers and sisters, whatever is true, whatever is noble, whatever is right, whatever is pure, whatever is lovely, whatever is admirable — if anything is excellent or praiseworthy - think about such things."*

So the word for you today is Let Go AND Hold On!

56

Time to Just MOW!

Many years ago while staying at my sister in England my uncles paid us one of many customary visits. One of the things they would do sometimes whenever they came over was mow the lawn. Like many homes in England my sister had a lovely garden with a lawn. However it was often necessary to cut it, because once the grass became overgrown and weeds started to grow up, it detracted from the beauty of the garden. Somehow my uncles always seemed to have the right mowing skills and we would stand aside and watch them tackle the lawn as they manoeuvred the lawnmower, but once they had accomplished their mission the garden looked refreshed and took on a new look. In our lives we too need to get into the MOWing business.

As human beings we are limited in what we can do, but with our limitations we still try to solve some problems that really are beyond our capabilities. The children of God are constantly targeted by the enemy but when the attacks come we need not fear. Instead we just need to Move Out of the Way and let God take over.

In 2 Chronicles 20:15, the Lord speaks through Jahaziel to encourage King Jehoshaphat, who is surrounded by a massive army, 'Do not be afraid or discouraged because of this vast army. For the battle is not yours, but God's."

He adds in verse 17,

> "You will not have to fight this battle. Take up your positions; stand firm and see the deliverance the Lord will give you . . . Do not be afraid; do not be discouraged. Go out to face them tomorrow, and the Lord will be with you.' "

This was after King Jehoshaphat acknowledged in verse 12, "*For we have no power to face this vast army that is attacking us. We do not know what to do but our eyes are on you.*" At their wits end, and admitting that they had no answer for the current problem the king and his people Moved Out of the Way and let God successfully fight the battle on their behalf for as Zechariah 4:6 reminds us it is, "*Not by might nor by power but by my Spirit,' says the Lord Almighty.*"

It's time for us to just MOW too - Move Out of the Way, keep our eyes on God and let Him, with His superior skills take over. Victory is assured.

57

In Piece/Peace or In Pieces

Whenever my husband cooks, (which is most of the time) he cleans as he goes along so that after serving and eating the meal there are just very few utensils to be washed. Before he taught me this however, I used to use the plates and cooking utensils, pile everything into the sink and then wash up after. His way is obviously much better because you have more time to sit in peace and relax after eating. Now imagine it's your birthday and you have just eaten one of the most delicious meals cooked by a family member. It is served on your finest china using the cutlery reserved for special occasions (personally I think you should use everything on any occasion). Everyone feels full and they feel happy. Everybody just wants to sit and relax in peace.

But wait just a minute! The dishes, cooking and eating utensils have to be cleaned up and someone has to do it. Someone who no doubt is feeling just as peaceful and full as you are at that time. After summoning all the will power they can muster someone trudges over to the sink to begin the arduous task. They really are not in the frame of mind and without warning a plate slips out of their hand, crashes to the floor and breaks into pieces.

At that moment all thought of the most delicious meal evaporates. They are so apologetic. You? Well it all depends. If you know God you could know that *"Peace of God, which passes all understanding,"* referred to in Philippians 4:7 which *"shall keep your hearts and minds through Christ Jesus."* However if you don't really know God then you will have no peace about the matter and like the plate your emotions will crumble and dissolve into pieces.

How we respond to the troubles of this world will affect our level of peace. When we are quiet, it gives us a chance to hear God's voice as He speaks. In Job 33:31 God tells Job, "*Mark well, O Job, hearken unto me: hold your peace and I will speak.*" Again in verse 33 God advises, "*Hold your peace and I shall teach you wisdom.*" In Proverbs 17:28 we are told that, "*Even a fool, when he holds his peace, is counted wise: and he that shuts his lips is esteemed a man of understanding.*" But how can we get this peace which so often seems to elude us?

In Isaiah 9:6 Jesus is referred to as the Prince of Peace and the prophet tells us in chapter 26:3 tells that God "*Will keep in perfect peace, him whose mind is steadfast, because he trusts in [Him]*" Psalm 119:165 posits, "*Great peace have they that love your law; and nothing can make them stumble.*" As we read and obey the word of God and keep our eyes and focus solely on Jesus we will grow in peace, though everything around us seems to be falling to pieces.

So are you in piece/peace or in pieces?

58

LOL

The other day one of my past students messaged me and in her note she used the abbreviations OFCC. Well I didn't have a clue what it meant and told her that at the risk of being laughed at I had to confess to her that I didn't know what it meant. She responded by telling me "Lol it means 'Of course'". My response was "IKT." I am not sure how many of you know what that means. I am not sure she did either, as she didn't respond. I was telling her "I Knew That," which is a phrase many students use in response to being given new information which they didn't know before! In these days of abbreviations and acronyms it helps if we are on the same page.

These days for many tech savvy people and those up-to-date with this new lingo that comes with text messaging when they see "LOL" they immediately think "Laugh out Loud," which is usually used in response to something that is deemed funny. Today the challenge is to view LOL in a different way. We hear so much about paradigm shifts, let us make one such shift with respect to Laughing out Loud, but not in response to something funny, but in response to the goodness of God and His blessings in our life.

Psalm 126:2-3 tells us, "*Then was our mouth filled with laughter, and our tongue with singing: then said they among the heathen, The LORD hath done great things for them. The LORD hath done great things for us; whereof we are glad.*" According to the Concise Oxford Dictionary[24] the word "glad" is defined as "*marked by, filled with or expressing joy*". It is God who has provided for us when we didn't know where provision would come from. Psalm 23:1 tells us "*The Lord is my Shepherd I shall*

---

[24] *Concise Oxford Dictionary 1990 8th Ed.*

not want," and in Philippians 4:19 we are told, *"But my God shall supply all your need according to his riches in glory by Christ Jesus."* It is He who has delivered us from some dark situations and has kept and preserved us. Psalm 121:7-8 emphasizes this. *"The LORD shall preserve thee from all evil: He shall preserve thy soul. The LORD shall preserve thy going out and thy coming in from this time forth, and even for evermore."*

It is God who has healed our bodies when we have been sick. It is He who paid the price for our sins and there is so much more that He has done for us and continues to do for us. So when we think of the goodness of God and what He has done for us we should be overjoyed. We should LOL - Laugh Out Loud and Love our Lord.

59

CB4C

What a strange topic - C Before C. You're probably scratching your head and wondering C before C? I'm sure you know your alphabet and know that C is C and so can't come before or after itself.

I have a number of friends who just love to watch the Miss World and Miss Universe Pageants. They soak in everything - the array of gowns, the "beauty" of the contestants, their walk, their answers to given questions and then they wait with bated breath for the results. Who will wear the prestigious crown? After the results, comes the debate and this is repeated year after year.

But I doubt whether very few stop to think about the rigours of these competitions. What we see on TV is the culmination of many months and sometimes years of work. Those contestants - the winner and the also rans - endure a lot prior to making that initial walk along the stage on competition night, but any sacrifices made by them pale in comparison to the overwhelming joy felt when they are announced as a finalist, runner-up or the eventual winner.

So it is in the kingdom of God. There can be no crown without a cross, the symbol of trials and sacrifice. In Luke 9:23 Jesus said to His disciples, "*If any man will come after me, let him deny himself, and take up his cross daily, and follow me.*" He reiterates this in Luke 14:27, "*And whosoever does not bear his cross, and come after me, cannot be my disciple.*" Just like all the contestants in the queen show endure serious training in the hope that they will wear the crown at stake, the one who follows Christ is assured of a reward and a crown that will last forever.

1 Corinthians 9:25 states, "*Everyone who competes in the games goes into strict training. They do it to get a crown that will not last, but we do it to get*

a crown that will last forever." Again in 1 Thessalonians 2:19 Paul says, *"For what is our hope, our joy, or the crown in which we will glory in the presence of our Lord Jesus when he comes?"*

It is not only in the dictionary that "Cross" comes before "Crown" but in our everyday practical walk with God it must be CB4C - Cross Before Crown.

Are you up to the challenge?

60

No Child Left Behind[25]

In 2001 the United States House of Representatives and Senate passed the No Child Left Behind bill which became law in January of the following year. The Act sought to "close the achievement gap with accountability, flexibility, and choice, so that no child would be left behind." Where a school's performance is repeatedly poor, according to the law, steps MUST be taken to improve the institution.

This can range from students voluntarily transferring to another school, schools offering free tutoring to struggling students, staff being replaced, implementing a new curriculum, extending instructional time, closing the school or hiring a private company to run the school. Over the years the "No Child Left Behind" slogan has become the watchword for educational officials in countries outside of the US aiming to improve teacher accountability and pupil performance.

The concept of No Child Left Behind, however, was established long before US lawmakers enacted this legislation. God was the originator of the idea. In John 3:16-17, we are told,

> *"For God so loved the world that He gave His only begotten Son, that whosoever believes in Him should not perish, but have everlasting life. For God sent not His Son into the world to condemn the world; but that the world through Him might be saved."*

It is God's desire that all are saved and that none is left behind or outside of His kingdom and for this reason He sent His son, Jesus

---

[25] *Wikipedia Internet Reference* accessed 4th September 2015

Christ. In John 6:40, Jesus states, *"For my Father's will is that everyone who looks to the Son and believes in him shall have eternal life, and I will raise them up at the last day."* Those who fail to accept the invitation though will face dire consequences. John 3:36 warns, *"Whoever believes in the Son has eternal life, but whoever rejects the Son will not see life, for God's wrath remains on them."*

This is certainly not an invitation to pass up on and it is one to be shared with others - family members, friends, work colleagues, neighbours, and acquaintances. Simply put EVERYBODY. It is important that not one of God's children is left behind and God is counting on those of us who have already accepted Him as Lord and Saviour to spread the word. Will you?

61

SIN

I recall many times over my teaching career when students were asked to define a word some would start with the word followed by the phrase "is when". I would always correct them and say something can't be "is when" forcing them to rethink and restate their definitions. However, today I am going against what I have always been instructing to say:

SIN is when you are:

Seriously In Need as a result of the Situation you are IN because your Soul Is Neglected and Salvation/a Saviour Is Necessary. It can be likened to a parked car where you are Sitting In Neutral and you are not going anywhere. And we all are guilty of it. The Bible has much to say on the topic: "*For all have sinned, and come short of the glory of God;*" Romans 3:23 KJV

> "*Let the wicked forsake his way, and the unrighteous man his thoughts: and let him return unto the Lord, and He will have mercy upon him; and to our God, for he will abundantly pardon.*" Isaiah 55:7 KJV

> "*If we say that we have no sin, we deceive ourselves, and the truth is not in us. If we confess our sins, He is faithful and just to forgive us our sins, and to cleanse us from all unrighteousness.*" 1 John 1:8-9 KJV

> "*For the wages of SIN is death; but the gift of God is eternal life through Jesus Christ our Lord.*" Romans 6:23 KJV

62

Give Me The FLAB!

It is said that as you get older it is more difficult to lose weight. These days it seems like everyone wants to get rid of unwanted pounds. Many have taken to all types of exercise - walking, running, cycling, going to the gym - while decreasing their food intake. Others who have tried these things with limited success have opted for the seemingly more effective gastric bypass instead. But if you talk to doctors they will tell you that having some flab or fat on your bones can actually be a good thing. Some become so obsessed with not putting on weight that they take such drastic measures and go to the next extreme, sometimes ending up with anorexia and/or bulimia. It is then that doctors and family members become so concerned with the person's health that they will try any means within their power to fatten up the 'victim" and restore some of the body mass.

God has plenty of FLAB in store for us and He wants to give it to us liberally. The fact that it is coming from God means it is good, for the Bible says, "No good thing will He withhold from those who walk uprightly." So what is God's FLAB like? It is His Favour, Loving kindness, And Blessings. In both the Old and New Testament God offers His FAVOUR. In Leviticus 26:3,9 it is a reward for obedience, "If you follow my decrees and are careful to obey my commands,... I will look on you with favour." And it is not limited for in 2 Corinthians 6:2 we learn that, "Now is the time of God's favour." In his ode to God, the Psalmist David acknowledges in Psalm 33:5 and 36:5,7 that, "The earth is full of [God's] unfailing LOVE, which, "reaches to the heavens," and is "priceless!"

AND God's promise of an abundance of BLESSINGS is found in Ezekiel 34:26, "I will send down showers in season; there will be showers *of blessing."* We learn more about the potential of these blessings from Proverbs 10:22, written by Solomon, regarded as the wisest man that ever lived, *"The blessing of the Lord brings wealth and He adds no trouble to it."*

Now if that is the kind of FLAB God is offering, I don't mind having it at all. Do you?

63

Just Go For It!

Do you know how many persons have conquered Mount Everest? No? Don't worry, neither do I, but I do know that many people have. One thing that we can agree on is that climbing a mountain is no easy feat and it is not a task for the physically or mentally weak. Climbers spend years preparing themselves. However the thrill of exhilaration on reaching the top surpasses any challenges met along the way.

Part of the poem, "Try Again[26]," says:

> *"Standing at the foot, gazing at the sky,*
> *How can you get up if you never try?*
> *Though you stumble off*
> *Never be downcast*
> *Try and Try again*
> *You'll succeed at last."*

To get to the top you can't just stand at the bottom and look up. You have to get to climbing upwards. There is no doubt that it is easier to ask God to remove the mountain, but climbing it builds character and fortitude and sometimes that's what God wants to do in us. Before a hurdler can be in contention for the gold medal he must clear every barrier before him.

The obstacles we face - and they are many and varied - may be intimidating, but be comforted by the word spoken by the prophet Jeremiah in Jeremiah 42:10-11,

---

[26] *Try Again taken from THE BEACON THIRD READER by* James H. Fassett *with a copyright dated 1914*

"If you stay in this land, I will build you up and not tear you down; I will plant you and not uproot you . . . Do not be afraid of the king of Babylon, whom you now fear. Do not be afraid of him, declares the Lord, for I am with you and will save you and deliver you from his hands."

Knowing that the King of the universe is with us every step of the way we just need to go for it and keep climbing.

64

Sticks and Stones

Have you ever looked back over your life and thought that there were many things you did as a child that now seem so silly and naïve? I remember repeating this jingle, "Sticks and stones may break my bones but words can never harm me." Oh how wrong I have discovered that saying is, for words do hurt. They are indeed powerful and can harm or help you. How you use them will determine where they will fall on the spectrum.

To use anything effectively you first have to learn how to do so. It took me three driving tests before I got my licence and several years more before I learnt to ride a bike! But I stuck to it and now I can do both, whether equally well is another matter.

The only way we can put the word of God to good use is if we read, learn and inwardly digest it so that we can use it readily and effectively when we need to, for according to Psalm 119:105, *"[God's] word is a lamp to [our] feet and a light to [our] path."* In acknowledging that *"our fight is not against flesh and blood but against the rulers, against the authorities, against the powers of this dark world and against the spiritual forces of evil in the heavenly realms,"* (Ephesians 6:12) the apostle Paul in Ephesians 6:17 advises us to, *"Take the helmet of salvation and the sword of the Spirit, which is the word of God."* Hebrews 4:12 describes the word of God as *"Living and powerful, and sharper than any two-edged sword, piercing even to the division of soul and spirit, and of joints and marrow, and is a discerner of the thoughts and intents of the heart."* The all-powerful sword of the living God is able to cut through every defense our enemy can raise. When wielded by God's servant, nothing can withstand its ability to cut straight to the core of a matter and uncover the truth.

As soldiers in God's army, it is our responsibility and duty to use His Word to discern the truth and then follow it. When God's Word shows us something wrong in ourselves, we can use this spiritual weapon to "surgically" remove the offending thoughts and actions.

2 Corinthians 10:4-5 posits that,

> *"The weapons we fight with are not the weapons of the world." On the contrary, they have divine power to demolish strongholds. We demolish arguments and every pretension that sets itself up against the knowledge of God, and we take captive every thought to make it obedient to Christ."*

God's word can cut through ANY defense the enemy can present. James 4: 7 tells us, *"Submit yourselves, then, to God. Resist the devil, and he will flee from you."* In Matthew 4: 4, 7, and 10 when Jesus was tempted by the devil He resisted his adversary by using the word, emphatically stating from the outset that, *"Man shall not live by bread alone but by every word that proceeds out of the mouth of God."*

Now if Jesus used the word to overcome temptation, how much more should we?

65

How Salty Are You?

"You can put in, but you can't take out." This was the advice my dad gave me many years ago as I was about to add some salt to ingredients which I had placed in a saucepan in preparation for cooking the day's meal. This was after I had asked him how much salt to put in. He explained that if I put in too much salt while cooking, I couldn't take it out and the food would become unpalatable because of its saltiness. On the other hand, if I didn't put in enough salt the food could be deemed tasteless by some, but fortunately more could be gradually added to enhance the taste.

These days, with hypertension and the threat of strokes (the silent killer) being linked to having diets too rich in salt (sodium), many persons opt to reduce their salt intake by using natural herbs instead to flavor their food. Salt, however, is also an excellent preservative and for many years was an effective agent in slowing the decay of meat and other foods so that they could be edible for a longer period. It is significant that Jesus likens us, His followers, to salt.

In Matthew 5:13 He says, "*You are the salt of the earth.*" Jesus used salt to describe how Christians are needed to bring balance and hope to an otherwise dying world. We must seek to "flavor the world," to effect positive change, to make a difference in the world, especially if we desire to follow Him. When we obey God and do His will we also act as a preservative of the human race by slowing down the moral and spiritual decay around us. We can also use our words to season or benefit those we talk to.

Colossians 4:6 tells us, "*Let your speech always be with grace, as though seasoned with salt, so that you will know how you should respond to each person.*" Note though that Jesus also intimates that we can lose our saltiness and this is what we need to guard against. *"But if the salt loses its saltiness, how can it be made salty again? It is no longer good for anything, except to be thrown out and trampled underfoot"* (Matthew 5:13b).

We must guard against becoming diluted by what is going on around us. How we react to our circumstances can have a positive or negative impact on our effectiveness. We can let our trials get the better of us and become less seasoned or we can use them to become more flavourful. How salty are you?

66

It's Time to FOG

In some tropical territories where the Aedes Aegypti mosquito is prevalent, authorities employ a method called fogging to help eradicate them. This involves driving through districts with a machine which emits a smoke-like substance (fog), containing chemicals, purportedly harmless to human beings, but designed to kill this insect, the carrier of dengue fever, chikungunya and yellow fever viruses, which can be fatal.

During the exercise residents are encouraged to open their windows and doors so that the chemically-laden fog can reach mosquitoes as it penetrates every nook and cranny where they might be hiding, because although people may not always see them they are there. They have a distinct sound, leave behind tell-tale bite marks on the skin and eventually full-blown symptoms become very evident.

This method is therefore ideal for permeating hard-to-reach areas such as gullies which are prime hiding and breeding grounds for the mosquitoes. The aim is to eradicate this dangerous insect before it can multiply and cause an epidemic. Satan and his angels are just like these mosquitoes. If left unchecked they will continue to breed and wreak havoc on humanity.

John 10:10 warns us that, *"The thief comes only to steal and kill and destroy."* Based on current events there can be little doubt that the devil is on a rampage. It is clear that we are in the last days as outlined by Matthew 24,

> *5"For many will come in my name, claiming, 'I am the Messiah,' and will deceive many. 6You will hear of wars and rumors of wars, 7Nation will rise against nation, and kingdom against kingdom.*

There will be famines and earthquakes in various places. ⁹Then you will be handed over to be persecuted and put to death, and you will be hated by all nations because of me. ¹⁰At that time many will turn away from the faith and will betray and hate each other, ¹¹and many false prophets will appear and deceive many people. ¹²Because of the increase of wickedness, the love of most will grow cold. ²⁴For false messiahs and false prophets will appear and perform great signs and wonders to deceive, if possible, even the elect. . . . ³³Even so, when you see all these things, you know that [the end] is near, right at the door. ³⁴Truly I tell you, this generation will certainly not pass away until all these things have happened. ³⁵Heaven and earth will pass away, but my words will never pass away."

As Christians we need to adopt a similar fogging method. We need to get the word out, to ALL places, by all means.

People need to know that Jesus is the Saviour of the world. In so doing we would be following Jesus' mandate in Acts 1:8 by being, His *"witnesses in Jerusalem, and in all Judea and Samaria, and to the ends of the earth,"* so that, *"This gospel of the kingdom will be preached in the whole world as a testimony to all nations,"* (Matthew 24:14). Desperate times require desperate measures, so spruce up your fogging gear. It's time to fog in earnest, to disseminate the message: Follow/Fear Only God!

67

Draw, AIM and Shoot!

Every time a crime is committed involving guns, there is plenty of talk in the media about banning them.

Some argue that guns are a necessity, while others posit that this weapon is not the real issue but the problem is with it falling into the hands of the wrong people - criminals who use them during the commission of crimes, curious children and sometimes adults who have not been properly trained how to handle them, persons with low self-esteem who deem themselves to have been rejected and want to get even with perceived offenders etc.

If a gun were to be pointed at you, it would be logical to assume that it was loaded and the immediate reaction would be to retreat. However, if somehow you knew that it was not loaded, your level of fear would diminish as without bullets the gun would be incapable of causing the kind of harm it could were it to have the right ammunition. God has given us a gun as well, a spiritual one, that is. The question is, Is yours loaded? The sword of the spirit which is the word of God forms part of the spiritual armour referred to in Ephesians 6:10-17.

In Proverbs 3:1 we are encouraged to, *Forget not [God's] law but let [our] hearts keep [His] commandments."*

Our heart is like our own gun. The question at hand: is it loaded? It is useless if it is not. For it to be effective against the devil it needs to be filled with the right firepower, the word of God. The only way we can do that is if we spend time reading the word daily and committing it to memory as the word is our resistance against the devil. James 4:7 advises us to, *"Resist the devil, and he will flee* from [us]." Each time the devil comes to test us we need to draw our loaded 'gun', take aim and shoot and we need to be persistent because he will keep advancing. In John 1:1 we learn that, *"In the beginning was the Word and the word was with God and the word was God."* When we load our hearts with the word we are loading ourselves with the power of God with which we can take aim and fire successfully at the target before us for 1 John 4:4 says, *"Greater is He that is within us than he that is in the world."*

So is your spiritual gun loaded? If so draw, aim and shoot!

68

Blind Man's Bluff

In years gone by, "Blind Man's Bluff[27]" was a popular game played by children at parties. While there are several versions of this game, the one with which I am most familiar, was where one child was tagged to be "It". The aim of the game was to tag another person while blind folded. After being spun around a few times the "blind man" would try to identify another child by feeling their face. If they did so correctly the identified person became "IT." Not only was it hilarious at times but often it could be frustrating especially when you couldn't guess the identity of persons and you had to keep going. At those times the person just gave up and someone else volunteered to be "IT."

It never ceases to amaze me how persons who are literally blind or partially sighted entrust their lives to someone else or to a guide dog. There is almost total reliance on the person or the animal that becomes their sight as they help them to get around accomplishing some of the simple tasks that sometimes we take for granted, such as crossing the street or grocery shopping. We could learn a lot from the bond formed between person and person or person and dog. It is one built on mutual trust.

Sometimes the challenges of life temporarily blind us and we become frustrated when we cannot "see" a way out. We need not be discouraged because the God of the universe is better than any helper or guide dog. In Isaiah 42:16 He assures us that He will,

---

[27] *Wikipedia Internet reference* accessed 14th September 2015

"Lead the blind by ways they have not known, along unfamiliar paths I will guide them; I will turn the darkness into light before them and make the rough places smooth. These are the things I will do; I will not forsake them."

God will reveal it to us in His word for as we read and study it, it will become, *"A lamp unto [our] feet, and a light unto [our] path"* (Psalm 119:105). Because we cannot see the answer in the natural, it does not mean that it does not exist. God sees it and knows it and we are expected to believe it. We need to follow the words of St Paul in 2 Corinthians 5:7 and, *"Live therefore by faith - "The substance of things hoped for, the evidence of things not seen"* (Hebrews 11:1) - *and not by sight."*

69

B or V

In the Spanish language the sound of the letters B and V are virtually interchangeable. Because of this some native Spanish speakers struggle with spelling some words, often substituting V's for B's in their writings. For example the word "vaca" which means "cow" would sometimes be incorrectly written as "baca". While the pronunciation remains the same the spelling is different and though students may argue that the meaning is the same they are always encouraged to rewrite the word correctly.

Sometimes, however, substituting one letter for another can change the meaning of a word altogether. In verse 25 of Nehemiah 9 the prophet reports that the Israelites, "*Captured fortified cities and fertile land; . . .took possession of houses filled with all kinds of good things, wells already dug, vineyards, olive groves and fruit trees in abundance. . . ate to the full and were well-nourished; they REVELLED in [God's] great goodness.*"

From this verse we learn that the Israelites enjoyed the blessings from God (reVelled). But then in the following verse we are told that, "*They were disobedient and REBELLED against [God] . . . turned their backs on [His] law. . . killed [His] prophets, who had warned them in order to turn them back to [Him]; . . . committed awful blasphemies.*" As a result of this change in behaviour, [27]"*God delivered them into the hands of their enemies, who oppressed them.*"

The change from a "V" in "revel" to a "B" in "rebel" changes everything completely. In Chemistry we are taught that for every action there is an equal and opposite reaction and for every type of behaviour there is a consequence, be it positive or negative. If we are obedient to God we will be well rewarded. Psalm 84:11 states, "*The*

Lord bestows favour and honour; no good thing does He withhold from those whose walk is blameless." Sometimes we find ourselves in untenable situations because we rebel against God instead of revelling in His goodness.

Fortunately, according to Nehemiah 9:31, *"In [God's] great mercy [He does] not put an end to [us] or abandon [us] for [He is] a gracious and merciful God."* 1 John 1:9 states clearly, *"If we confess our sins he is faithful to forgive us our sins and cleanse us from all unrighteousness."*

So reVel - not reBel.

70

Unbelievable

They often say that seeing is believing but if you have ever watched the TV show, Ripley's Believe It Or Not[28] you may question the truth of that statement. The events that are portrayed are often so bizarre and the items so strange and unusual that viewers often doubt what they are actually seeing and whether these sometimes preposterous things actually took place.

When we read some of the events that are recorded in the Bible they too seem absolutely astounding, but they are real. In Genesis chapter 1 God created the heaven and the earth - day and night, the heavens, the sky, the sea and land, trees, animals, birds and sea creatures, the moon, the sun and the stars and finally the first man and woman and all of this at the sound of his voice. Throughout the chapter we read, "*And God said. . .*" and it was done! How else can we describe these feats but simply amazing!

In Exodus 14:21-22 God parted the Red Sea as a means of escape for the children of Israel,

> "*And the LORD caused the sea to go back by a strong east wind all that night, and made the sea dry land, and the waters were divided. And the children of Israel went into the midst of the sea upon the dry ground: and the waters were a wall unto them on their right hand, and on their left.*"

His power is also demonstrated in 1 Kings 18:38, "*Then the fire of the LORD fell and burned up the sacrifice, the wood, the stones and the soil, and also licked up the water in the trench.*"

---

[28] *Ripley's Believe It or Not* Internet Reference 16th September 2015

The Bible is replete with many instances of God's mighty power, but there are many who would want to discount not only His existence but His awesome power. Numbers 23:19 assures us that, *"God is not a man, that he should lie, nor a son of man, that he should change his mind. Does he speak and then not act? Does he promise and not fulfill?"*

We serve an incredible God, one who is able to do *"exceeding abundantly above all that we ask or think,"* (Ephesians 3:20). Now isn't that just unbelievable?

71

High Fives

According to Wikipedia, the "**high five[29]**" is a "hand gesture that occurs when two people simultaneously raise one hand each, about head-high, and push, slide, or slap the flat of their palm against the flat palm of the other person. The gesture is often preceded verbally by a phrase like "Give me five" or "High five." It can be used as a greeting but is best associated with congratulations or a celebration of some sort usually after some spectacular feat has been achieved.

Adults also encourage children to "Give me five" when they have done something outstanding and the gesture is not only an acknowledgement that something spectacular has been achieved but it also acts as extrinsic motivation for individuals to continue to do well.

When we consider God's goodness to us each instance can only be considered as a High Five moment. Deuteronomy 28:1 states, "*If you fully obey the LORD your God and carefully follow all his commands I give you today, the LORD your God will set you high above all the nations on earth.*"

In Psalm 18 David extols the greatness of God. Here is some of what he says about the Lord,

> *[2]The LORD is my rock, my fortress and my deliverer; my God is my rock, in whom I take refuge, my shield[b] and the horn[c] of my salvation, my stronghold.[3] I called to the LORD, who is worthy of praise, and I have been saved from my enemies.[16] He reached down from on high and took hold of me; he drew me out of deep*

---

[29] *Internet Reference* accessed 17th September 2015

waters.[17] He rescued me from my powerful enemy, from my foes, who were too strong for me.[18] They confronted me in the day of my disaster, but the LORD was my support.[28] You, LORD, keep my lamp burning; my God turns my darkness into light.[29] With your help I can advance against a troop[e]; with my God I can scale a wall.[32] It is God who arms me with strength and keeps my way secure.[33] He makes my feet like the feet of a deer; he causes me to stand on the heights.[34] He trains my hands for battle; my arms can bend a bow of bronze.[39] You armed me with strength for battle; you humbled my adversaries before me.[40] You made my enemies turn their backs in flight, and I destroyed my foes.[43] You have delivered me from the attacks of the people; you have made me the head of nations.

Read the entire chapter and you will see the magnificent feats which are attributed to God. He is more than worthy of a high five. Give Him Five!

72

From PR to PA

Abbreviations, abbreviations, abbreviations! Depending on the context they mean different things to different people. In the Cayman Islands for example, PR refers to Permanent Residence, the right conferred on non-Caymanians to remain in the Cayman Islands for the rest of their life. On the other hand PA in some places could mean Personal/Personnel Assistant or even Public Address as in PA system.

In library catalogues the above letters could refer to the beginning part of a book's title or its author. Usually though PA would appear first. Today I want to talk about a Biblical character who was treated most unfairly, but who rose to great acclaim in the land of Egypt. That person was Joseph. His story is one of hope in the midst of adversity after adversity. Here is a brief outline of his journey as found in Genesis chapters 37 and 39-50

1. His brothers hated him and plotted to kill him.
2. They sold him into slavery at the age of 17.
3. His father was made to believe that he was dead.
4. He was falsely accused of sexual assault.
5. He was stripped from his position of privilege and thrown into prison
6. A possible early release from prison was not realized because of a broken promise.
7. He is remembered for his ability to interpret dreams and is brought from prison.

8. He gives Pharaoh the interpretation of his dream and is elevated to second in command. (Now aged 30!)

9. He saves his family from sure death as a result of the famine.

10. He sees his brothers for the first time in 21 years.

11. At 39 years he reveals himself to his brothers and

12. Eventually he is reunited with his dad.

As you read his story the one phrase that resonates throughout the chapters is: *"But the Lord was with Joseph."* At no point was he ever alone. He may have been away from his home and family and familiar surroundings but he was not alone. God was with him.

There are lots of lessons to be learnt from Joseph's situation but two of the most important would have to be maintaining a good attitude (ouch) and being quick to forgive. We may not always understand why we are experiencing the trials, the heartache, the injustice etc. but be reminded of Joseph's response to his brothers in Genesis 50:20, *"You meant evil against me, but God used it for good."*

God is the same yesterday, today and forever and whatever He has done before He can do again. You could be like Joseph and literally or figuratively go from PR to PA., from PRison to PAlace.

73

Stuck At The Traffic Lights?

Red Light, Green Light, One, Two, Three! I remember playing this traffic light game a long time ago where one person turned their back and stood a little distance away from the other players. He/she would shout, "Red Light, Green Light, One, Two, Three" before turning around. The aim of the game was to reach and touch the player while their back was turned without being caught. The first person to do so was the winner and took their place. Anyone who was caught advancing was sent back to the original starting point to begin again. It was exciting to see players trying to outwit each other as they tried to maneuver their way. Fortunately the thought of any danger was non-existent unlike that posed by a motorist's failure to follow real traffic light signals. This reminds me of the time I was driving my sister's vehicle a few years back.

As I approached the traffic lights the red signal illuminated which meant I should stop. I did so and awaited the green light to continue. Just as I was about to drive off in accordance with the signal my sister cautioned me to wait as there was now a new trend where persons were driving through the red light. Sure enough someone did. I was appalled, but have since realized that the trend is quite common. These days it seems like most motorists are in a desperate hurry to reach their destination in as short a time as possible.

Drivers have become so impatient that should a fellow motorist pause too long at the green light there is an immediate honking of the horn.

Despite the increase in the number of traffic accidents - some of them fatal - as a result of running a red light, more and more persons continue to do so. Exodus 23:2 cautions us, *Do not follow the crowd in doing wrong."* It doesn't matter if everyone is doing it wrong is wrong. In Proverbs 14:12 we are warned that, *"There is a way that appears to be right, but in the end it leads to death."*

Today a growing number of persons continues to alienate God and engage in unsafe practices which will ultimately lead to their eternal death. We need to be a part of that group who will obey the traffic signs set by God himself in His word. Even if no one is doing it right is still right. Matthew 7:13-14 advises,

> *"Enter through the narrow gate. For wide is the gate and broad is the road that leads to destruction, and many enter through it. But small is the gate and narrow the road that leads to life, and only a few find it."*

Stuck at the traffic lights? Obey the signs CORRECTLY!

74

"Mind the Gap!"

If you have ever travelled on the British Underground Railway system you may have heard this expression being repeated as commuters board and/or disembark from the train. It's a word of warning to railway users to help safeguard them against falling between the area between the platform and the train which could be potentially fatal. There are even markings painted on the ground advising you not to step beyond a certain line while awaiting the train. Sometimes adults can be seen pointing out the boundary lines to each other and their children. This is similar in some ways to how God operates.

He gives us guidelines and throughout time He has commissioned people to not only warn mankind about the imminent dangers associated with sin and going beyond the boundaries which He has set, but to intercede on their behalf before Him. The prophet Ezekiel was one such person. In Ezekiel 22:30, God tells the prophet, "*I looked for someone among them who would build up the wall and stand before me in the gap on behalf of the land so I would not have to destroy it, but I found no one.*" It is an awesome responsibility but think of the commendation to be received from God himself. "*Those who are wise will shine like the brightness of the heavens, and those who lead many to righteousness, like the stars for ever and ever*" (Daniel 12:3). We are fast running out of time and there is no time to procrastinate any longer. Luke 10:2 tells us that, "*The harvest is plentiful, but the workers are few. Ask the Lord of the harvest, therefore, to send out workers into his harvest field.*"

Fanny Crosby sums it up beautifully in her song, "Rescue the Perishing"[30]

---

[30] *Rescue the Perishing*, Fanny Crosby 1869

Rescue the perishing, care for the dying,
Snatch them in pity from sin and the grave;
Weep o'er the erring one, lift up the fallen,
Tell them of Jesus, the mighty to save.

Refrain:
Rescue the perishing, care for the dying,
Jesus is merciful, Jesus will save.

Though they are slighting Him, still He is waiting,
Waiting the penitent child to receive;
Plead with them earnestly, plead with them gently;
He will forgive if they only believe.

Down in the human heart, crushed by the tempter,
Feelings lie buried that grace can restore;
Touched by a loving heart, wakened by kindness,
Chords that were broken will vibrate once more.

Rescue the perishing, duty demands it;
Strength for thy labor the Lord will provide;
Back to the narrow way patiently win them;
Tell the poor wand'rer a Savior has died.

We need to echo the refrain to those who need to hear it,

"Mind the Gap!"

75

Yes, It Is!

"When Jesus says 'Yes', nobody can say, 'No'." [31]

This line from a chorus sums up Jesus' response concerning every prayer that we have prayed and every promise that He has made.

2 Corinthians 1:19-22 tells us,

> *"For the Son of God, Jesus Christ…was not "Yes" and "No," but in him it has always been "Yes." For no matter how many promises God has made, they are "Yes" in Christ. And so through him the "Amen" is spoken by us to the glory of God. Now it is God who makes…you stand firm in Christ. He anointed us, set his seal of ownership on us, and put his Spirit in our hearts as a deposit, guaranteeing what is to come."*

It doesn't matter how long our answer seems to be in coming it is on its way for God watches to see that His word is fulfilled (Jeremiah 1:12) and the word that goes out from His mouth does not return to Him empty, but accomplishes what He desires, and achieves the purpose for which He has sent it (Isaiah 55:11).

Our task is to declare the promises of God over our lives and the lives of our loved ones and keep pressing in until we receive what His word says belongs to us. In Genesis 32:26, Jacob demonstrates the kind of tenacity that is needed. He wrestled with the angel of God all night long, refusing to let go, declaring boldly instead, *"I will not let you go unless you bless me."* And boy was he blessed!

---

[31] *When Jesus says Yes* Michelle Williams, 2014

As long as we obey God's commandments He will bless us too and give us the desires of our heart according to His will. Psalm 84:11 tells us, *"For the Lord God is a sun and shield; the Lord bestows favor and honor; no good thing does He withhold from those whose walk is blameless."*

Don't be disheartened, however, as a delayed response to prayer does not necessarily mean a denial. God is looking for people who will become desperate enough to take their faith to a higher level. Remember, the woman with the issue of blood (Luke 8) waited 12 years for her miracle while the man at the pool of Bethesda waited 38 years for his. They were yearning for a miracle and they got one. God has *not forgotten you. Whatever you are believing God for your miracle IS on the way. Yes, it is!*

76

Outnumbered

My husband and I are ardent soccer fans. Sometimes while watching a match, a player from one of the teams is sent off. You would think that with an extra player the team holding this advantage would totally dominate the game but this is not always the case. Somehow the team-mates of the red-carded player take their game to a higher level, which always prompts my husband to say, "Ten always play better than eleven."

It is not a given that the team with its full complement will win because sometimes the game ends in a draw and occasionally the disadvantaged side even wins! Sometimes the daily challenges of life make us feel like we are outnumbered but that doesn't have to spell defeat for us. In the books of 1st and 2nd Kings both Elijah and his successor Elisha found themselves at times outnumbered.

In 1 Kings 18: 22 the prophet Elijah laments, "*I am the only one of the Lord's prophets left, but Baal has four hundred and fifty prophets.*" In his quest to get the people to repent and acknowledge the Lord as the one true God, Elijah issues a public challenge to the prophets, "*You call on the name of your god, and I will call on the name of the Lord* (v. 24). *The god who answers by fire — he is God.*" Elijah prayed to God and the Lord answered with fire causing the people to exclaim, "*The Lord — he is God!*" The 450 false prophets were then captured and killed. Later, in 2 Kings 6: 15-17, when the king of Aram sent his men to capture Elisha, the prophet's servant was scared when he saw the size of the army surrounding the city and said to his master, "*Oh no, my lord! What shall we do?*"

In response Elisha says, "*Don't be afraid. Those who are with us are more than those who are with them,*" and then he prayed, "*Open his eyes, Lord, so that he may see.*" The Bible says that the LORD opened the servant's eyes, and he looked and saw the hills full of horses and chariots of fire all around Elisha. That day, after Elisha prayed to God, from a position of seemingly certain victory the King's army was struck with blindness and led by the prophet like sheep to the slaughter into the city of their enemies. In both instances the difference between victory and defeat lay in the fact that God was fighting on the side of the underdog.

Always remember whenever you feel outnumbered that one with God is a majority and hence victory is assured.

77

The Promise

I remember as a child growing up that my playmates and I would share secrets with each other. We solemnly swore not to reveal any information deemed "sacred", often sealing our pledges with the words, "I promise. Cross my heart and hope to die!" It didn't take long before the "secret" was passed on from one person to another until eventually many people knew. Oh how naïve we were back then! As I got older and supposedly much wiser I adopted a different attitude and whenever someone would say, "I promise," I would cynically retort, "A promise is a comfort to a fool."

Understandably, this response wasn't always well received. One day, however, I was forced to reconsider, when a dear friend shared with me that my response was incomplete as the ending should in fact be, "But a guarantee to a friend." This changed my mindset.

Unlike my childhood acquaintances, I learnt that day that there are friends who can be trusted to keep their promises, even though they may also disappoint us at times. There is one person however, who is the epitome of what a true friend should be - loyal, honest, trustworthy, faithful, true, selfless - and that person is Jesus.

In John 15:13-15 He tells us,

> *"Greater love has no one than this: to lay down one's life for one's friends. You are my friends if you do what I command. I no longer call you servants, because a servant does not know his master's business. Instead, I have called you friends, for everything that I learned from my Father I have made known to you."*

Here are some of the promises that He has shared with us:

> *"And being fully persuaded that, what He had promised, He was able also to perform."* Romans 4:21

> *"And if ye be Christ's, then are ye Abraham's seed, and heirs according to the promise."* Galatians 3:29

> *"The promise is for you and your children and for all who are far off – for all whom the Lord our God will call."* Acts 2:39

> *"In hope of eternal life, which God, that cannot lie, promised before the world began."* Titus 1:2

> *"Let us hold fast the profession of our faith without wavering; (for He is faithful that promised ;)"* Hebrews 10:23

> *"Blessed is the man that endureth temptation: for when he is tried, he shall receive the crown of life, which the Lord hath promised to them that love Him"* James 1:12

> *"The Lord is not slack concerning His promise, as some men count slackness; but is longsuffering to us-ward, not willing that any should perish, but that all should come to repentance."* 2 Peter 3:9

> *"Nevertheless we, according to His promise, look for new heavens and a new earth, wherein dwelleth righteousness."* 2 Peter 3:13

> *"And this is the promise that He hath promised us, even eternal life."* 1 John 2:25

And these promises can't and won't be broken! At least not by God!

78

God Will

In the English language the words *"shall"* and *"will"* often suggest the future. *"Will[32]"* is derived from Old English *"willan"* meaning *"to want or wish"* and is related to the Latin words *"velle"* (*"wish for"*) and *"voluptas"* (*"pleasure"*), and the Polish *"woleć"* (*"prefer"*). They all suggest *"to wish for or desire."* Though both forms are used interchangeably to express the future the use of *"will"* often carries different connotations. It can express habitual action, willingness, desire or intention or the likelihood or expectation of something happening.

When we declare that "God will" we are saying that beyond any shadow of a doubt He causes whatever it is that we are believing Him for, to come to pass, no matter how the situation may appear to us at the present time. If we are really desperate to have God act on our behalf we need to declare authoritatively that "God will..." and we will see the answers to our prayers. He prefers and is more than willing and desirous to do it, we can expect Him to, it is highly likely that He will and it gives Him great pleasure to fulfill our requests.

So declare now: God will...

> ... hear   Micah 7:7 *"But as for me, I watch in hope for the LORD, I wait for God my Savior; my God will hear me."*
>
> . . . act   Genesis 50:24 *"God will surely come to your aid."*

---

[32] *Wikipedia Internet Reference 25th September 2015*

. . . deliver   2 Kings 17:39 *"Rather, worship the Lord your God; it is he who will deliver you from the hand of all your enemies."*

. . . heal   Matthew 8:8 *"Lord, I do not deserve to have you come under my roof. But just say the word, and my servant will be healed."*

. . . comfort   Jeremiah 31:13 *"I will turn their mourning into gladness; I will give them comfort and joy instead of sorrow."*

. . . forgive   Isaiah 55:7 *"Let the wicked forsake their ways and the unrighteous their thoughts. Let them turn to the LORD, and he will have mercy on them, and to our God, for he will freely pardon."*

. . .establish   Deuteronomy 28:1 *"If you fully obey the LORD your God and carefully follow all his commands I give you today, the LORD your God will set you high above all the nations on earth."*

. . .provide   Philippians 4:19 *"And my God will meet all your needs according to the riches of his glory in Christ Jesus."*

. . .prepare the way (close doors, open doors) Psalm 59:10 *"God will go before me."*

. . . fight for us   Nehemiah 4:20 *"Our God will fight for us!"*

. . . care   Psalm 9:18 *"But God will never forget the needy; the hope of the afflicted will never perish."*

. . . keep and protect   Joshua 1:9 *"Do not be afraid; do not be discouraged, for the LORD your God will be with you wherever you go."*

. . . save   Isaiah 35:4 *"Be strong, do not fear; your God will come, He will come with vengeance; with divine retribution He will come to save you."*

. . . restore and return   Deuteronomy 30:3, *"The Lord your God will restore your fortunes."*

. . .favour and bless   Deuteronomy 15:6 *"For the LORD your God will bless you as He has promised, and you will lend to many nations but will borrow from none."*

. . . sustain   Psalm 55:22 *"Cast your cares on the Lord and he will sustain you; He will never let the righteous be shaken."*

AND most importantly:

God will . . .

NOT FAIL   Luke 1:37 *"For no word from God will ever fail."*

God will!

79

On The Alert

Sometimes while walking along the corridors on my way to class, I would pass several students just sauntering along. In an effort to get them to speed up occasionally I would say to those heading towards my lesson, "Anyone who gets there after me will get a detention." Immediately most of them start walking faster, but sometimes - just to add some drama and a little bit of humour - without warning I would start to run, prompting some of them to take off running as well, all in an effort to stay ahead of me. One or two of the stragglers though, are caught off-guard, and when they realise what is happening they too try to make a dash for it, but their reaction time is too slow and they scamper in vain.

Every one of us is in the fight of our lives and we have to stay on the alert. God is fighting for our souls but so too is His/our enemy, the devil. 1 Peter 5:8 warns us, "*Be alert and of sober mind. Your enemy the devil prowls around like a roaring lion looking for someone to devour.*" Again in Ephesians 4:27 we are cautioned, "*Do not give the devil a foothold.*" When the prophet Nehemiah sought to rebuild the walls of Jerusalem he and the people supporting him met with stiff opposition spearheaded by Sanballat and Tobiah.

Here is what we are told in chapter 4 of his book,

> ⁷"*But when Sanballat, Tobiah, the Arabs, the Ammonites and the people of Ashdod heard that the repairs to Jerusalem's walls had gone ahead and that the gaps were being closed, they were very angry. ⁸They all plotted together to come and fight against Jerusalem and stir up trouble against it. ¹¹Also our enemies said,*

"Before they know it or see us, we will be right there among them and will kill them and put an end to the work."

The builders did not flinch however.

Here was their reaction,

> [9]*"But we prayed to our God and posted a guard day and night to meet this threat.* [16]*From that day on, half of my men did the work, while the other half were equipped with spears, shields, bows and armor. The officers posted themselves behind all the people of Judah* [17] *who were building the wall. Those who carried materials did their work with one hand and held a weapon in the other,* [18]*and each of the builders wore his sword at his side as he worked.* [21]*So we continued the work with half the men holding spears, from the first light of dawn till the stars came out.* [22]*At that time I also said to the people, "Have every man and his helper stay inside Jerusalem at night, so they can serve us as guards by night and as workers by day."* [23]*Neither I nor my brothers nor my men nor the guards with me took off our clothes; each had his weapon, even when he went for water."*

And that is how we too should be - On the Alert constantly!

80

The Voice[33]

Viewed by millions of people around the world this very popular reality TV show, which started about 4 or 5 years ago, features contestants who are aspiring singers drawn from public auditions. There are usually 4 stages of the competition: Blind Auditions, in which four renowned recording artists/coaches, listen to the contestants in chairs facing opposite the stage so as to avoid seeing them. If a coach likes what they hear from that contestant, they press a button to rotate their chairs to signify that they are interested in working with that contestant. If more than one coach presses their button, the contestant chooses the coach he or she wants to work with.

The coaches dedicate themselves to developing their singers mentally, musically and in some cases physically, giving them advice, and sharing the secrets of their success. Next comes the Battle Rounds, where the coaches put two of their own team members against each other to sing the same song together in front of a studio audience. In some versions, the winners of the battle rounds proceed to the Knockout Rounds. As in the battle rounds, coaches pit two of their own team members to compete against each other. This time, the contestants choose their own song to perform individually while the other watches and waits. After that, the coach chooses one to advance while the other is sent home. At the end of the knockout rounds, the strongest members of each coach's roster proceed to the Live Stage shows. In this final performance phase of the competition, the top

---

[33] The Voice *Wikipedia Internet Reference* accessed 27th September 2015

contestants from each team compete against each other during a live broadcast.

The television audience vote to save one contestant on each team, leaving the coach to decide on live television who they want to save and who will not move on. In the next round, the public chooses between the two artists left on each team, and the coach also has a vote that weighs equally with the public vote. Finally, each coach will have his/her best contestant left standing to compete in the finals, singing an original song. From these four, one will be named "The Voice"—and will receive the grand prize of a recording contract. Feelings of pride, ecstasy, sheer delight and gratitude reverberate everywhere and for a long time after, the winner of the Voice is the topic of conversation.

But the Bible speaks about another VOICE which is far better than the winner's and that of the coaches. It is one which directs us to God. Isaiah makes reference to it in Isaiah 40:3, "*A voice of one calling: "In the wilderness prepare the way for the Lord; make straight in the desert a highway for our God,*" and the writer of Hebrews advises us, "*Today when you hear [God's] voice, don't harden your hearts as Israel did when they rebelled*" (Hebrews 3:15).

According to Revelation 3: 20 we are all invited to have an audition with Jesus, the King of Kings and the Lord of Lords, and a positive response will generate feelings much greater than those felt after the winner of the reality programme is announced and will be worth a whole lot more than a recording contract! "*Behold, I stand at the door and knock. If anyone hears My voice and opens the door, I will come in and eat with that person, and they with me.*" There are no losers with a yes vote with Jesus. So listen to and follow HIS VOICE, THE VOICE!

81

The Present

"Nothing like a present!"

I have always been excited about receiving gifts. As a child at Christmastime, I used to be so excited that I would try to take a sneak peak of my wrapped presents before Christmas Day arrived. Of course when the day came, opening the gifts was the first thing on my mind. After unwrapping the presents my brother and I liked to show off our gifts to each other. Now that I am grown, however, the excitement of receiving gifts has waned and now there is no rush to open them.

But there is one present that surpasses any that I could ever have received and it is reflected in the song, "Special Delivery[34]" which speaks about God's unselfish gift of His Son Jesus Christ to mankind:

Never was anyone like Him, never will one be the same
Tiny babe, an Infant King, Saviour, we worship and honor the
power of His name

Chorus:
He came special delivery, wrapped up in love, bound by a
promise, sealed by a dove

And filled with the spirit, carried by grace, you knew where He
was goin', by the look on His face.

This gift has been described in 2 Corinthians 9:15 and James 1:17 respectively as "*indescribable*" and "*good and perfect.*" It will not be forced on you but is available on request and should not be ignored.

---

[34] *Special Delivery YouTube Internet Reference* accessed 28th September 2015

Matthew 7:11 tells us, "*If you, then, though you are evil, know how to give good gifts to your children, how much more will your Father in heaven give good gifts to those who ask him!*" 2 Corinthians 6:2 advises us, "*Behold, now is the accepted time; behold, now is the day of salvation.*" It is a gift for which we should be eternally grateful but how we respond to it will have everlasting consequences for each of us. Romans 6:23 tells us, "*For the wages of sin is death, but the gift of God is eternal life in Christ Jesus our Lord.*" So what will you do with the present?

82

Behind or in Front?

Does it really matter? For some people it does. One of my pet peeves is to be bypassed by someone standing behind me,while waiting in line to be served. As far as I am concerned if they are behind they should just await their turn. It reminds me of a funeral I went to once. In the church's graveyard you couldn't help but notice a huge metal cross with a number of graves in front and behind it. Apparently the tradition was that if you were not a communicant or a member of the church you would be buried behind the cross.

On the other hand communicants and church members were buried in front of it. How ironic and a bit judgmental! The cross a symbol of salvation and refuge is being used by people who are called by God to judge others who cannot speak in their defence. It is evident that this divisive practice defies the command of Matthew 7:1, "*Judge not, that ye be not judged.*" Fortunately this custom cannot in any way determine the eternal destiny of anyone. 1 Samuel 16:7 tells us that, "*The Lord does not look at the things people look at. People look at the outward appearance, but the Lord looks at the heart.*"

While it is always better for persons to commit their hearts to God at the earliest opportunity according to Ecclesiastes 12:1, "*Remember your Creator in the days of your youth, before the days of trouble come and the years approach when you will say, "I find no pleasure in them,"* even at the hour of death should someone repent of their sins and ask Jesus to come into their dying heart, He is merciful and will forgive and save. Romans 10:13 assures us, "*For whosoever shall call upon the name of the Lord shall be saved.*" So behind or in front? Does it really matter? Not really. It's where you are in God that matters the most.

83

It's The Fan Life[35]

My husband and I are ardent premier league soccer supporters and on Saturdays we just relish sitting home and watching game after game. I always marvel at my husband's ability to quote soccer statistics so accurately. A few years ago we decided to actually go to a real live game and so we planned a trip to England. As part of the preparations, which started months in advance, once we had decided which game we were going to attend, we reserved our seats, booked a flight and a nearby hotel and purchased the match tickets on line.

We even decided to do a tour of the grounds on the day after the match. It was a costly affair but we enjoyed it immensely. Just to ensure that we knew how to get to the stadium we checked into the hotel the day before and took a leisurely stroll down to the match grounds that evening. On the day of the match we were literally one of the first to get there and we took our seats - we had an excellent vantage point - and waited for over an hour before the start of the match! We were well prepared for the weather as well. I was bedecked in my gloves, jacket and scarf! Once the match began the euphoria was tremendous. We took pictures, screamed and cheered along with the other 76000 + fans. Fortunately our team won but it didn't really matter to us (well yes it did) but just being there was delight enough.

The next day we took a tour of the locker room, the field and the museum and climaxed our trip with the purchase of lots of memorabilia. (I have since given away most of mine.) Incredible how we will go to such lengths to enjoy the pleasures of this world which will eventually fade away, but sometimes struggle with the

---

[35] Jentezen Franklin *Sermon Real Fans YouTube* accessed 16th March 2014

things of God which are more meaningful than anything this life has to offer. Matthew 6:33 advises us to, *Seek first the kingdom of God and His righteousness, and all these things will be given to you as well."* The Psalmist David makes his position clear in Psalm 84:10, *"Better is one day in your courts than a thousand elsewhere; I would rather be a doorkeeper in the house of my God than dwell in the tents of the wicked."*

We too need to develop a fan mentality when it comes to the things of God. 1. Be enthusiastic. *"Bless the Lord, O my soul: and all that is within me, bless his holy name"* (Psalm 103:1). 2. Attend church regularly, be on time and be excited about going. *"I was glad when they said unto me, Let us go into the house of the Lord"* (Psalm 122:1). 3. Memorise the scriptures. *"Bind them about thy neck; write them upon the table of thine heart"* (Proverbs 3:3). 4. Pay your tithes and offerings to help finance the kingdom of God. *"Bring the whole tithe into the storehouse, that there may be food in my house"* (Malachi 3:10). 5. Be vocal in your worship to God. *"O clap your hands, all ye people; shout unto God with the voice of triumph"* (Psalm 47:1).

Now that's the life of a real fan. Are you a real fan of God?

84

Inhale/Exhale?

How long can you hold your breath for? Sometimes when my husband and I go to the beach we compete against each other to try to see how long we can hold our breath for underwater. As you near the point when you just simply must exhale you start to feel so uncomfortable - as if you would burst - but still you try to hold out. Eventually you just can't take it anymore and you have to take that breath of fresh air. And does it feel good! Some people seem to have lungs with an extraordinary capacity to hold oxygen for a long time! Free fall divers are some such folk and maybe it comes with practice.

But I am sure you will agree that regardless to how long you can hold your breath for, at some point you have to exhale and inhale again or you will simply die. Harbouring unforgiveness and bitterness is like holding your breath beyond what is bearable. When you refuse to let go of these feelings it can lead to discomfort - emotional, psychological and sometimes physical (psychosomatic) - and the longer you stay in "inhale" mode the more uncomfortable you will feel. You may have heard the saying, "To err is human, but to forgive is divine[36]." Forgiving those who have wronged you is a must and taking a decision to put the feelings of hurt behind you is like a breath of fresh air, but true forgiveness cannot be achieved in our own might. It can however be obtained with God's help.

Plus if you don't forgive others when they have wronged you, God won't forgive you when you need it. Matthew 6:14-16 states it quite plainly, "*For if you forgive men when they sin against you, your heavenly*

---

[36] Alexander Pope 1688-1744

Father will also forgive you. But if you do not forgive men their sins, your Father will not forgive your sins."

This is also reiterated in Mark 11:25: *"And when you stand praying, if you hold anything against anyone, forgive him, so that your Father in heaven may forgive you your sins."*

So how long can you hold your breath? It's time to exhale.

85

Front, Rear or All-Wheel Drive[37]

I salute all those persons who can tell the difference between a front wheel and rear wheel drive vehicle. What matters to me most is that my car is functioning and that it can get me from point A to point B! However, according to car manufacturers and car enthusiasts the front wheel drive vehicle is considered superior to the rear wheel drive one especially in wet weather or conditions such as snow or mud as it improves the grip of the tyres in such conditions.

It is advisable that persons with powerful cars opt for rear wheel drives because weight transference under acceleration reduces the weight on the front wheels and reduces their traction, which is an important factor in reducing wheel spins.

Although the skill of a driver is a significant factor in controlling any vehicle, knowing the type of wheel drive can determine the type of response a driver would make in the event of their car going out of control. Knowing what to do can help to avoid accidents and possible injury. Thank goodness we serve a God who has exceptional "driving" skills, is always in control and is not caught unaware by situations and changes in circumstances.

According to Philippians 3:21 God has *"The power that enables Him to bring everything under His control,"* and 2 Chronicles 25:8 reiterates that *"God has the power to help or to overthrow,"* and it is *"His divine power [that] has given us everything we need for a godly life through our knowledge of Him* (2 Peter 1:3).

---

[37] *Wikipedia Internet Reference* accessed 3rd October 2015

"That power is the same as the mighty strength He exerted when He raised Christ from the dead and seated him at His right hand in the heavenly realms, far above all rule and authority, power and dominion, and every name that is invoked, not only in the present age but also in the one to come" (Ephesians 1:19-21).

There is no need to fear with God in control for, *"Great is our Lord and mighty in power; His understanding has no limit"* (Psalm 147:5).

He will surely bring every situation under control, for He is, *"The God who performs miracles, [who displays] His power among the peoples"* (Psalm 77:14). And *"He rules forever by his power, His eyes watch the nations"* (Psalm 66:7). In considering God's mighty acts of causing the waters of the Jordan river to recede and parting the Red Sea Joshua declares in Joshua 4: 24 that, *"He did this so that all the peoples of the earth might know that the hand of the Lord is powerful and so that you might always fear the Lord your God."*

When we allow God to be our driver He will steer us in the right direction and maintain control. He doesn't provide a front wheel or rear wheel drive. He is a combination of both. He's like an All-Wheel Drive.

86

Cat In The Mirror

Some years ago the late pop singer Michael Jackson penned the song "Man in the Mirror[38]." Here is the refrain to that popular song:

> *"I'm starting with the man in the mirror*
> *I'm asking him to change his ways*
> *And no message could have been any clearer*
> *If you wanna make the world a better place*
> *Take a look at yourself and then make that change."*

Seems like pretty straightforward advice but is it that simple to make a change after looking in the mirror? It depends on a number of factors: what you see, what you think you see, whether you accept the perception or the reality or whether you are committed and determined to making a change. It is said that when persons suffering from anorexia look at themselves in a mirror they see a fat person, while to the rest of the world they are just skin and bones.

The anorexics' perception causes them to continue starving themselves instead of seeking help and/or increasing their food intake. Compare that scenario to a picture I once saw in which a cat was admiring itself in the mirror. The reflection being depicted, though, was not that of a cat, but a strong, powerful, roaring lion! No doubt that the cat that sees itself as a lion will not allow itself to be intimidated by challenges faced but will approach these situations with the courage and the boldness of a lion. Do you know that when God created light He called it out of absolute darkness? He said, "Let there be! And

---

[38] *Man In The Mirror* Michael Jackson 1987

there was! What are you hoping for? What kind of change do you want to see? What mountains do you want God to surmount on your behalf?

God has already declared that we are *"the head and not the tail, above and not beneath"* (Deuteronomy 28:13) and *"more than conquerors"* (Romans 8:37), so we should not be daunted by what we see with our natural eyes for God is able to do *"exceedingly abundantly above all that we ask or think,"* (Ephesians 3:20).

1 Corinthians 1: 25, 27-28 tell us that

> *"The foolishness of God is wiser than human wisdom, and the weakness of God is stronger than human strength. But God chose the foolish things of the world to shame the wise; God chose the weak things of the world to shame the strong. God chose the lowly things of this world and the despised things - and the things that are not — to nullify the things that are."*

The phrase *'But God'* suggests that despite what we are experiencing in the natural when God intervenes there is a complete reversal.

Our present circumstances cannot negate God's promises and declarations over our life. Like the cat in the photo what we believe can determine our responses and even our destiny. What we need to do is to focus less on the problems confronting us and start visualizing and praising God more for the breakthroughs that await us. Mark 11:24 posits, *"Therefore I tell you, whatever you ask for in prayer, believe that you have received it, and it will be yours."* The omnipotent God, the source of all wisdom can make a way out of what seems to us to be no way, for as Romans 4:17 reminds us, we serve a God who, *"Gives life to the dead and calls into being things that were not."* So, how do you see yourself? Hopefully like that cat in the mirror.

87

Say No to Nits

Many years ago while staying at a host family during an overseas trip I encountered a lovely little girl. She was a very pretty, pleasant and well-mannered child. I sat her down on my lap but no sooner had I done this than my hostess cautioned me to put her down as she was suspected of having lice!

I was taken aback but promptly obeyed and as the child sat away from me, though difficult to see at first, my hostess pointed out these very tiny crawling white things in her hair which they referred to as the nits. Fortunately they had not been transferred to my hair! This was clearly a case of all that glitters not being gold! I was reminded of this incident recently when I came across the expression "nitpicking." It was referring to the act of finding fault with every minute and sometimes insignificant detail, a practice of which I have to admit I have been guilty. Simply put it is being critical about any and everything.

Unfortunately it is not often constructive criticism and many times inaccurate opinions which are usually negative are formed about individuals. Ephesians 4:29 warns us, "*Do not let any unwholesome talk come out of your mouths, but only what is helpful for building others up according to their needs, that it may benefit those who listen.*" Having a critical spirit therefore does not help, but hinders and will only lead to grieving the Holy Spirit. What we need to do instead is follow the advice of 1 Thessalonians 5:11, "*Therefore encourage one another and build up one another.*" In this way we can avoid being robbed of God's blessings. We can only be successful if we do not conform to worldly patterns, endeavouring instead to change our mindset.

Romans 12:2 instructs us, *"Do not conform to the pattern of this world, but be transformed by the renewing of your mind. Then you will be able to test and approve what God's will is--His good, pleasing and perfect will."* This is reiterated in 1 Peter 3:10, *"Whoever would love life and see good days must keep their tongue from evil and their lips from deceitful speech."*

"Instead, speaking the truth in love, we will grow to become in every respect the mature body of him who is the head, that is, Christ" (Ephesians 4:15). To do this we must simply Say No to Nits!

88

Rescued

I enjoy eating fish, but I have to say I hardly give a thought to what a fisherman has to endure when he goes fishing to catch this delicacy to put on our dining tables. There have been many instances when these seafarers have encountered difficulties or been lost at sea while plying their trade. Sometimes it happens without warning and they lose contact with those on shore. It is then that they have to keep their wits about them and maintain their courage as they use their experience and skills in order to survive.

Many a survivor and their family members will tell you that they never lost faith that their loved one would be rescued and sometimes although it looked like all hope was gone they were rescued. The pain and discomfort of the ordeal is replaced with the ecstasy of having been found. There is no feeling like being pulled to safety. On the other hand there have been instances where fishermen have been presumed lost at sea and the pain of this presumption never seems to ease for those left behind. We may not have fishermen in our families but we are surrounded by people who are in danger of being eternally lost and we have our part to play in saving them. Jesus calls us to be fishers of men and there is immense joy when we have been instrumental in rescuing any of them.

The Bible tells us in Luke 15:7, "*I tell you that in the same way there will be more rejoicing in heaven over one sinner who repents than over ninety-nine righteous persons who do not need to repent.*" The time is now according to 2 Corinthians 6:2, "*I tell you, now is the time of God's favor, now is the day of salvation.*" Oh to be rescued!

89

Bargains Galore!

One of my very dear friends once gave me a bag with this inscription, "I'd rather shop than eat." It really is a pretty good description of me as I really enjoy shopping. Unlike in years gone by though when I just bought things just for the sake of buying them, now I purchase what I need and I try to get as much as I can for as little as possible, but it does take time, I have to admit... I love a bargain and so do many people I know. Give-aways are even better!

While I have never done many of these things, it's amazing what some people will do to get bargains and giveaways though. Some will actually camp out overnight, form extraordinary long lines, collect vouchers, climb on top of others, lose their temper and even fight. Anything just to get that so called ideal item which is so great in demand and which they think they can't possibly do without. It is ironic that after so much time and energy have been expended in acquiring this stuff sometimes after a few uses it is discarded. Worse yet when it doesn't live up to its billing and there is no warranty!

What is even more ironic though and sad, is that there are still many people in this world today who continue to ignore the greatest bargain and give-away of all time with a guaranteed warranty and an excellent return on service. First of all, it's an offer given freely by Jesus. *"Everyone who calls on the name of the Lord will be saved"* (Romans 10:13). Should you accept, your sins will be completely blotted out *"Though your sins are like scarlet, they shall be as white as snow; though they are red as crimson, they shall be like wool"* (Isaiah 1:18). Next, whatever you lose will be restored to you. *"And everyone who has left houses or brothers or sisters or father or mother or wife or children or fields for my sake will receive a hundred times as much and will inherit eternal life"* (Matthew 19:29) and *"Whosoever will lose his life for my sake shall find it"* (Matthew 16:25).

Finally, there are better things in store.

> *"My Father's house has many rooms; if that were not so, would I have told you that I am going there to prepare a place for you? And if I go and prepare a place for you, I will come back and take you to be with me that you also may be where I am"* (John 14:2-3).

What a bargain!

90
Which Way?

When it comes to directions I am very poor. I rarely ever (more like never) venture out to new places on my own as I have a deep seated fear of being lost. Some years ago while on an overseas netball trip my team and I visited a large outdoor flea market. It was big and imposing.

My husband, who accompanied us, suggested that I use the simple straightforward system of walking down one row and then up the other. He clearly advised me against flitting from side to side. However, I became so captivated by the merchandise on offer that it didn't take me long to abandon his advice and I just kept walking wherever my eyes would lead me. Before long I had lost sight of the group and I was alone. I had no idea where I was nor did I know which way to go. I found myself in a situation I have always dreaded - being lost. And then I started to panic. I started walking around aimlessly trying to find my way back to my team mates.

Shopping was now the furthest thing from my mind. After what seemed like a long time - too long it seemed - I heard my husband calling my name. He had found me! I was so relieved I started to cry. Of course he reprimanded me for not following his instructions, but I didn't mind. I was safe. While my being lost was only temporary, we are living in a world where many people are jeopardizing their eternal safety every day. They are lost and they do not know which way to go, seemingly oblivious to the dangers that await them. Psalm 1:6 states, *"For the LORD watches over the way of the righteous, but the way of the wicked leads to destruction."*

There are still others who believe that there are many roads to God but they too are fooling themselves, for Jesus states categorically in

John 14:6, "*I am the way and the truth and the life. No one comes to the Father except through me.*" Perhaps you already know the way, but **do you know persons who are lost and don't know which way to go?** Then it's your duty to point them to Jesus, who reminds us in Mark 2:17, that "*[He has] not come to call the righteous, but sinners to repentance,*" assuring us in Luke 15:7 that, "*There will be more rejoicing in heaven over one sinner who repents than over ninety-nine righteous persons who do not need to repent*".

91

Get Out of Jail Free

As a child growing up, my family played the Milton Bradley board game Monopoly[39] a lot. The game, which involves buying and selling property can go on for hours on end and sometimes we would start the game one day and continue it the next. I remember one Christmas we were entertaining some other family members and my mum was roasting peanuts. We were all so engrossed in the game that we forgot the nuts until we smelled them burning!

One of the challenges of this game is to avoid being "sent to jail" which means you are temporarily deprived of participating except of course for collecting rent should someone land on property you have bought. However, if previously you had been fortunate enough to "pull" a "Get Out of Jail Free" card you could trade it in at any point while in jail and gain your "freedom". All playing privileges are then immediately restored. Oh, what a relief! Life is somewhat like that Monopoly game although the consequences are permanent and could be a lot more dire.

We have all been born prisoners to sin: Psalm 51:5 informs us, *"We have all been born in sin and shaped in iniquity."* This point is reiterated in Romans 3:10 and Romans 3:23 respectively, *"There is no one righteous, not even one;"* and, *"For all have sinned and fall short of the glory of God."*

As a result we have been sentenced not to 'jail' but death. *"For the wages of sin is death"* (Romans 6:23).

Many too are very engrossed in their sin. There are some also, who, believe that living a "good" life and performing good deeds is enough

---

[39] *Wikipedia Internet Reference Monopoly* Milton Bradley

to earn them the right to escape this punishment, but according to Ephesians 2:8-9, their belief could not be further from the truth,

> *"For it is by grace you have been saved, through faith — and this is not from yourselves, it is the gift of God — not by works, so that no one can boast."*

1 John 1:10 also posits,

> *"If we claim that we have not sinned, we make him a liar, and his word is not in us."*

We can get out of "jail" free though, but that provision can only come through Jesus Christ. Romans 5: 19 advises, **"For just as through the** *disobedience of the one man the many were made sinners, so also through the obedience of the one man the many will be made righteous."* This latter one man is Jesus who holds the get out of jail free card with which He promises everlasting life: *"The gift of God is eternal life in Christ Jesus our Lord"* (Romans 6:23).

92

What Scent Are You Wearing?

I love a good perfume, so much so that there was a time in my life that I actually had a different perfume for each day of the month and I still used to buy more! But that is a practice I have long ago abandoned, choosing instead to use what I have before adding to the already clustered dresser.

A few weekends ago while sitting in the airport on my way back home a lady came and sat beside me. The fragrance she was wearing was so overwhelming that I couldn't resist telling her that it was really very nice. She thanked me, said it was called Burberry and then went on to explain that she had sprayed it generously over the coat she was wearing to hide its musty smell as a result of it being in a drawer for a long period of time. I knew exactly what she was referring to and assured her that the perfume had indeed done a great job! I have no doubt though that the odour might still have been there but the perfume had acted as a very good cover up.

Sometimes in life we try to mask our "scents" by saying and doing the "right things in the right places." How we behave on the job, while driving on the streets, on the playing field, behind closed doors or in our private lives, identifies who we really are. However, while we may try to fool people we cannot fool God, for according to Luke 8:17, "*Nothing is secret, that shall not be made manifest; neither anything hid, that shall not be known and come abroad.*" We also learn in 1 Samuel 16:7 that, "*The LORD does not look at the things people look at. People look at the outward appearance, but the LORD looks at the heart.*"

As children of God, we need to let the light of God radiate from us all the time, both publicly and privately.

According to Matthew 5:14-16,

> *"You are the light of the world. A town built on a hill cannot be hidden. Neither do people light a lamp and put it under a bowl. Instead they put it on its stand, and it gives light to everyone in the house. In the same way, let your light shine before others, that they may see your good deeds and glorify your Father in heaven."*

So, what scent are you wearing?

93

Is Your Antenna Working?

One of the most frustrating things for me is manually trying to locate a channel on one of those little portable radios. Sometimes when I think I have it, I hear the voices from another channel coming through instead. I have often been told, "You need an antenna" or in the case when I did have one, "Your antenna is not working properly." This piece of equipment, technicians will tell you, is often necessary to ensure that radios, TVs and other electronic devices work well and give you a much better reception.

It is incredible how the sound and/or picture quality is so enhanced just by simply adding this instrument. The idea of antennae is nothing new though as when God created insects he endowed them with these appendages as their primary olfactory sensors. They use them to smell out things ranging from food to danger. Human beings have also been gifted with antennae in the form of their 5 senses. When one or more of them are lost however there is overcompensation by the remaining ones. Despite this occurrence, however, God has made available to everyone of us, a divine antenna which allows Him to communicate with us. Sometimes though there is so much interference around us that it is difficult for us to recognize His voice and hear Him clearly when He is speaking. We need to find ourselves a quiet place and tune into God's frequency so that we can listen to Him clearly. Reading and meditating on His word is a good starting point. It can't be just coincidental that the same letters that spell 'listen' also spell "silent." Habakkuk 2:20 advises us, "*The LORD is in his holy temple; let all the earth be silent before Him.*"

When God's intermediary, Moses, addressed the children of Israel in Deuteronomy 27:9 the first thing he told them was, "*Be silent, Israel, and listen!*" A very common joke about teachers goes like this: Who keeps on talking when no one is listening? The answer: A teacher. If we were to substitute teacher with God I don't think we would consider it funny or a joke, but it is a sad reality.

In Luke 9:35, after Jesus' baptism, God not only acknowledged Him as His son but commanded that we listen to Him. "*This is my Son, whom I have chosen; listen to him.*" In Hebrews 1:1-2 we are told, "*In the past God spoke to our ancestors through the prophets at many times and in various ways, but in these last days he has spoken to us by his Son.*" We need to listen to the voice of God, but more importantly we need to do what it tells us to. "*Do not merely listen to the word, and so deceive yourselves. Do what it says*" (James 1: 22).

So how well is your antenna working?

94
Soft or Hard

Did you know that water may be classified as being hard or soft? It's a rather strange term to describe this vital commodity but one which is easy to explain. According to one blogger the major difference between hard and soft water can best be seen while doing household chores. I quote,

> Hard water is to blame for dingy looking clothes, dishes with spots and residue and bathtubs with lots of film and soap scum. Even hair washed in hard water may feel sticky and look dull. Hard water can take a toll on household appliances as well, using up more energy. The elements of hard water are to blame for all of these negative factors, as soap is less effective due to its reaction to the magnesium and calcium. The lather is not as rich and bubbly[40].

Simply put, it is more difficult dealing with hard water than it is with soft water. Let's examine our speech using this same analogy.

Our words can have a positive or negative effect depending on whether they are "soft" or harsh. The Bible says in Proverbs 15:1, "*A soft answer turns away wrath, but a harsh word stirs up anger.*" Sometimes in the heat of the moment we may utter words which are harsh and hurtful. Like hard water such words are difficult to manage, leaving stains behind, for once they have been uttered we cannot pull them back. That is why it is important to think before you speak. On the other hand, Proverbs 25:11 advises us that, "*A word fitly spoken is like*

---

[40] *Internet Reference* accessed 20th October 2015

199

apples of gold in pictures of silver." Many a soft word will quench a potential "firestorm".

Hear the words of James 3:5-10,

> "*Likewise, the tongue is a small part of the body, but it makes great boasts. Consider what a great forest is set on fire by a small spark. ⁶The tongue also is a fire, a world of evil among the parts of the body. It corrupts the whole body, sets the whole course of one's life on fire, and is itself set on fire by hell. ⁷All kinds of animals, birds, reptiles and sea creatures are being tamed and have been tamed by mankind, ⁸but no human being can tame the tongue. It is a restless evil, full of deadly poison. ⁹With the tongue we praise our Lord and Father, and with it we curse human beings, who have been made in God's likeness. ¹⁰Out of the same mouth come praise and cursing. My brothers and sisters, this should not be.*"

Finally according to Proverbs 18:21 "*The tongue has the power of life and death, and those who love it will eat its fruit.*"

Seems a daunting task trying to control our speech but here is a song (sung to the tune of Jingle Bells) that I learnt at VBS many years ago: "Watch your words, Watch your words, Careful what you say. Words can make a person sad, or make them smile all day. Watch your words, Watch your words, Think before you speak. Think of something good to say today and through the week." So are your words soft or hard? May the words of the song help to guide us as we seek to effect positive change through positive words.

95

Brother's Keeper

Am I my brother's keeper? This was Cain's retort to God after he had slain his brother, Abel and God had inquired after the latter. Many of us condemn Cain but how very much like him are we? I learnt recently of the passing of a former colleague. We studied for A levels together and then later at teachers' college and eventually we ended up teaching at the same school.

Some years ago, however, she became depressed and suffered a nervous breakdown and though she tried, she never really seemed to recover. Learning of her death was shocking and very sad and it caused me to do some serious introspection. My self-examination prompted me to admit that I had not been very good at being my "brother's" keeper. While we cannot be there physically for everyone who is experiencing some sort of challenge in their life or even lend financial support, what we can do is pray for them. James 5: 16 clearly states, "*Pray for each other so that you may be healed. The prayer of a righteous person is powerful and effective.*"

So my plea today is for us to consciously intercede on behalf of those who suffer from depression and mental illness. Let us be our brothers' and sisters' keepers by asking God to restore their minds. Perhaps because we are clothed in our right minds it is difficult for us to fully understand what torment they face on a daily basis, but nothing beats the power of prayer and with God all things are possible. He can heal and restore them. While it is easy to celebrate with people when things are going well let us also remember to stick by them when things are not going so well and whisper a prayer in the morning, at noon and at evening on their behalf. Let us be our brother's and sister's keeper.

Let us *"Rejoice with those who rejoice;* [but more importantly] *mourn with those who mourn."* Romans 12:15.

96

All That Glitters...

Have you ever "read" the book, "Everything Men Know About Women[41]" by Dr. Alan Francis? According to reports over one million copies have been sold of this book. I can attest to having bought two of them and one of my friends was gifted one by her principal when she got married. If you have ever bought or seen a copy then you know that on the back cover the author gives you a synopsis of what some of the chapters contain. Here is the real funny part though (depending on your sense of humour, that is): The book is a collection of blank pages! One person has actually uploaded a video on You Tube calling it the most stupid book ever. It may be stupid but the writer has sure made a pretty penny off of it. It really is a case of all that glitters not being gold!

Our daily life encounters with Satan are somewhat like that book. Referred to as the master of deception, the devil has the ability to present temptations and sin as wonderfully wrapped packages. Remember in Genesis 3:4 he tried to contradict God's word and coerced Eve into eating the forbidden fruit by telling her, "*You surely will not die!*" Well we all know that that was one of the first lies ever told and we are all still suffering as a result. Lest we think that we are immune from his schemes the apostle Paul tells us in 1 Corinthians 10:12, "*Wherefore let him that thinketh he standeth take heed lest he fall,*" and he goes on to warn us in 2 Corinthians 11:3, "*As the serpent deceived Eve by his craftiness, your minds will be led astray from the simplicity and purity of devotion to Christ.*" The reason why Satan can do this is because he has the ability to disguise himself as "*an angel of*

---

[41] *Everything Men Know About Women* Dr Allan Francis *1995*

light" (2 Corinthians 11:14), and according to 2 Corinthians 4:4, he has "*Blinded the minds of the unbelievers so that they cannot see the light of the gospel that displays the glory of Christ, who is the image of God.*"

I once heard a preacher say, "Sin will take you farther than you want to go, keep you longer than you intend to stay, and cost you more than you want to pay." Yielding to temptation can be very costly but there is hope. 2 Thessalonians 3:3 states, "*But the Lord is faithful, and He will strengthen and protect you from the evil one.*"

Again in 1 Corinthians 10:13 we are told,

> "*No temptation has overtaken you except what is common to mankind. And God is faithful; He will not let you be tempted beyond what you can bear. But when you are tempted, He will also provide a way out so that you can endure it.*"

Sugar and salt can both be white but it would be foolhardy to substitute one for the other based simply on their colour. Remember all that glitters may not be gold. It's better to take heed once you've been told.

97

Terra Firma

I enjoy Fridays immensely, primarily because it is the end of the work week and I look forward to going to the beach with my husband. We like to don our goggles which allow us to view the fish swimming below the surface which is so exciting and relaxing. My enjoyment at the sea nowadays though is a far cry from what it was like on my very first visit, many, many, many years ago.

I was about 8 or 9 years old. I remember because it was shortly after my mum relocated to Barbados from England and she had decided to take my brother and me to the sea, an activity which was new and foreign to us. As she led me to the water's edge I recall screaming and trying to run back as the sensation of the sand moving from beneath my feet as the water beat upon it, was terrifying for me. I had never experienced the "ground moving" from underneath my feet before and I was scared stiff. I did not enjoy my first visit at all. Some years later I was reminded about my "dilemma" by some people who later became my friends and who had been at the sea at the same time. They found it hilarious. I, not so much.

Over the years I have conquered most of my fear of the sea, even though I still refuse to go where I can't comfortably stand up, but that doesn't mean the ground isn't there to support me. I just need to overcome my fear. Trusting in God is somewhat like this. Sometimes we feel afraid. We feel as though He is not there because we don't seem to sense His presence. But like the ground, He is definitely there. He is a firm foundation. As the songwriter says, "On Christ the solid rock I stand, All other ground is sinking sand[42]." We need to learn to

---

[42] Hymn *My Hope is Built on Nothing Less*, Edward Mote 1834

trust Him implicitly. In Psalm 18:2 the Psalmist David refers to the LORD as, "*My rock, my fortress and my deliverer; my God is my rock, in whom I take refuge, my shield and the horn of my salvation, my stronghold.*" Whatever you are believing God for today, this is a reminder that He is not like the sand that moves beneath your feet when the water beats against it. When we call out to Him for His help, deliverance is guaranteed even when the situation seems bleak. We are reminded in Psalm 27:5, "*For in the day of trouble He will keep me safe in his dwelling; He will hide me in the shelter of his sacred tent and set me high upon a rock.*"

Let us follow the advice of the psalmist in Psalm 61:2 "*From the end of the earth will I cry unto thee, when my heart is overwhelmed: lead me to the rock that is higher than I.*"

That rock is Christ, our Terra Firma that cannot be moved.

98

Banker's Cheque or Rain Check

Every Thursday, one of the local supermarkets issues a flyer in the newspaper with specials for the coming week. The savings are tremendous and often some products are so popular that by the time you reach the supermarket the stock has been depleted. The supermarket owners in an effort to satisfy their customers will issue what is known as a "rain check" which enables you to purchase the item at the special price whenever next they are in stock, even if the time for the original concessions has expired. Sometimes though restocking can take a while, but their word is their bond and it is honoured. How much more is the word of God, the creator of the universe, honourable?

The fundamental difference between God and the supermarket though is that while the latter may run out of stock God will never do so and we can be assured that if He makes a promise to us He will fulfill it, even if what we are hoping for seems delayed. Numbers 23:19 tells us, *"God is not human, that He should lie, not a human being, that He should change his mind. Does He speak and then not act? Does He promise and not fulfill?"* Rather God's modus operandi is like that of presenting a banker's cheque. The funds are there and guaranteed but may take a while to clear. So when we feel like what we want is not forthcoming be reminded that God has our banker's cheque in His hand waiting to hand it over to us. Remember Jeremiah 29:11 tells us, *"For I know the plans I have for you,"* declares the Lord, *"plans to prosper you and not to harm you, plans to give you hope and a future."* So hold out your hand for that banker's cheque from God.

99

The Proof of the Pudding...

They say that the proof of the pudding is in the eating. Of course you can't attest to the real taste of anything unless you have tried it. You can't go by looks or even reviews. The best way is to prove it yourself.

The phrase 'finger-licking good" has been associated for years with Kentucky fried chicken, created by the late Colonel Sanders, but you know if you have never eaten his "masterpiece" you can't subscribe to his view. When I was much younger I used to lick not only my fingers but also the plate after I had a meal that I thoroughly enjoyed. I just didn't feel like I could get enough of it. While I don't engage in that practice now, (mainly because it is viewed as socially unacceptable) occasionally when at home I would take a slice of bread and sop up the gravy. My husband doesn't like to see it, but I try to justify this practice by telling him it is a testament to his good cooking!

Our relationship with God should be somewhat like that. We should yearn for and be so filled with Him that we feel as though we can't get enough. Think of how we act when there is a special person in our life. We want to speak to them at every available opportunity, see them whenever we can, be with them at the earliest convenience. That is how it should be with God and He is far better than "finger-licking good!" Psalm 16:11 tells us, "*In the presence of the Lord there is fullness of joy and at his right hand there are pleasures for evermore,*" and we are encouraged in Psalm 34:8 to, "*Taste and see that the LORD is good,*" for according to 1 Timothy 4:4, "*Everything created by God is good, and nothing is to be rejected if it is received with gratitude.*"

But you won't know unless you try Him for yourself. After all, the proof of the pudding is in the eating!

100

The Butterfly

"The heavens declare the glory of God; the skies proclaim the work of his hands" (Psalm 19:1). God's creations are absolutely amazing but the one I find so very unique is the butterfly. I don't recall ever seeing one that is not so delightfully beautiful and watching them can be so mesmerizing. When I consider this creature I can do nothing but marvel at the transformation that it undergoes. Butterflies have a typical four-stage insect life cycle. Winged adults lay eggs on plants on which their larvae, known as caterpillars, will feed.

These caterpillars look just like fat worms or grubs ambling slowly along. They keep growing until they are fully developed when they will pupate in a chrysalis. What they do is wrap themselves up in in what resembles a silky cotton covered pod. At this stage they are changing state and when this metamorphosis is complete, the pupal skin splits, the adult insect climbs out and, after its wings have expanded and dried, it flies off - now a gorgeous butterfly[43]! There is no resemblance whatsoever to the caterpillar. This incredible process, one that we cannot fully comprehend, speaks volumes of the majesty and omnipotence of God, who is an awesome miracle worker. Only He has the ability to completely change something or someone.

Bearing this in mind it doesn't matter what we used to do, where we used to go or who we used to be, when we have an encounter with Jesus Christ and we ask him to forgive us of past sins He completely transforms us. 2 Corinthians 5:17 clearly states, *"Therefore, if anyone is in Christ, the new creation has come: The old has gone, the new is here!"* Satan, however, will always try to remind us of our past and will

---

[43] *Wikipedia Internet Reference* accessed 27th October 2015

cause us to doubt who we are in Christ, but never forget that, "*God made Him (Christ) who had no sin to be sin for us, so that in Him we might become the righteousness of God*" (2 Corinthians 5:21) and because of this, "*There is now, therefore, no condemnation for those who are in Christ Jesus, . . . who walk not after the flesh but after the Spirit*" (Romans 8:1). Therefore when we consider the works of God's hands let us join the psalmist in Psalm 139:14 when he says, "*I praise you because I am fearfully and wonderfully made; your works are wonderful, I know that full well.*" And though our beginnings may be humble our future will be prosperous (Job 8:7).

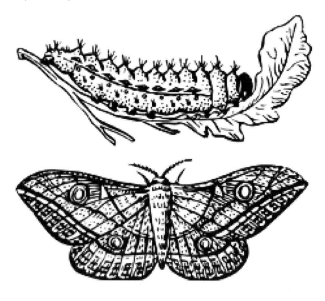

101

The Ayes Have It?

I am always amazed how the "aye" votes always seem to be in the majority, especially in parliamentary proceedings. It seems like motions to be passed are always so worded that persons can't help but vote "Aye." Although at times I have heard persons giving loud and emphatic "No's" this choice never seems to outweigh the other and invariably the speaker or the person presiding will shout after the voting process, "The Ayes have it!" But while the majority may vote "Yes" the majority is NOT always right and it seems that these days the Ayes don't have it. Many will use the Human Rights and Freedom of Speech arguments to justify wrong doing, but the "rightness" or "wrongness" of any action is determined by God's infallible word contained in His book the Bible and will ultimately be judged by Him and it doesn't matter who or how many are agreeing to it if according to that word, it is wrong then no amount of "Yes" votes will make it right.

In 1 Kings 22 when Jehoshaphat, king of Judah at the time was asked by Ahab, king of Israel to accompany him into battle against the king of Aram to reclaim property which he thought was rightfully theirs, the former responded by advising the latter to,

> *"First seek the counsel of the Lord."* Ahab brought together about 400 prophets who all suggested that he proceed with his planned action. Jehoshaphat remained unconvinced and obviously valuing God's word, asked whether there were any prophets of God of whom they could inquire. In his reply Ahab answered and said, *"There is still one prophet through whom we can inquire of the Lord, but I hate him because he never prophesies anything good about me, but always bad.*

He is Micaiah." He was rebuked by Jehoshaphat for saying this but despite this pronouncement Micaiah was sent for by a messenger, who not only told him what all the other prophets had said but advised him, to *"Let your word agree with theirs, and speak favorably."* Micaiah would not be swayed however and responded thus, *"As surely as the Lord lives, I can tell him only what the Lord tells me."*

To cut a long story short Micaiah advised the king not to go to war and was imprisoned as a result of his "dissenting" voice. God in fact caused a deceiving spirit to enter the mouths of the 400 prophets to entice Ahab, who followed the majority ruling and was sent to his demise. Let us learn from this story and not allow ourselves to be swayed by every form of doctrine.

Ephesians 4:14 advises us not to be like infants any longer, who are *"Tossed back and forth by the waves, and blown here and there by every wind of teaching and by the cunning and craftiness of people in their deceitful scheming."* Remember, WRONG is WRONG even if everyone is doing it and RIGHT is RIGHT even if no one is doing it. The "Ayes" don't always have it.

102

WHOA

I don't know how or when "Whoa" originated but it is the word of choice said to horses when you want them to slow down or stop. Many a horseman/horsewoman will shout it out as they yank the reins attached to the bit in the animal's mouth. I'm not sure why they don't just say, "Stop" though, but maybe "Whoa" is horse language for "Stop." Whatever the case it is clearly a word that many horses have been "taught." It is significant to note that there is tugging on the bit inside the mouth at the same time. While people don't wear such a contraption, at times, some of us, including me, would do well to adopt a "Whoa' attitude especially when it comes to speaking.

The proverb "Silence is Golden" perhaps was borne out of the following verses: Proverbs 10:19 English Standard Version, which cautions, *"When words are many, transgression is not lacking, but whoever restrains his lips is prudent,"* and 2 Timothy 2:16, *"Avoid godless chatter, because those who indulge in it will become more and more ungodly."* According to Ecclesiastes 3:1-8 God has ordained a time for everything under the sun, even speaking, *"There is a time for everything, and a season for every activity under the heavens . . . a time to be silent and a time to speak,"* but we need to learn when those times are.

Unfortunately the temptation to say something is often so great that we regularly falter. We can, however, learn a lot from the Psalmist David who sought God's help in this area, as he prayed in Psalm 141:3, *"Set a guard, O Lord, over my mouth; keep watch over the door of my lips!"* We may not be horses, but "Whoa!"

103

No Hay Rosas Sin Espinas

There are some who will tell you that carnations signify love but for many persons roses will definitely do the trick. Considered as the most perfect flower and with over 100 species varying in size and shape, the attractive flowers are usually large and showy in colours ranging from white through yellow to the most famous red[44]. I would venture to say that florists would regard this symbol of love as being the best seller of all.

I have a friend who signs her school emails with the Spanish phrase, *"No hay rosas sin espinas,"* which means, *"There can be no roses without thorns."* I find it interesting that the rose is so popular in spite of the fact that each stem comes bedecked with prickles. But there is more to this quote than its literal meaning. What it suggests to us is that nothing in life, that is good and worth having, comes easy and without enduring varying degrees of pain, but, the end is worthwhile. If you have ever been given roses and been pricked by one of the accompanying thorns you know it can be painful, but the thrill of receiving those roses just seems to overcome that discomfort.

In 2 Corinthians 12:7-10 the apostle Paul makes reference to a thorn that he had to contend with.

He says,

> [7]*"In order to keep me from becoming conceited, I was given a thorn in my flesh, a messenger of Satan, to torment me. [8]Three times I pleaded with the Lord to take it away from me. [9]But he said to me, "My grace is sufficient for you, for my power is*

---

[44] *Wikipedia Internet Reference* accessed 1st November 2015

made perfect in weakness." Therefore I will boast all the more gladly about my weaknesses, so that Christ's power may rest on me. [10]That is why, for Christ's sake, I delight in weaknesses, in insults, in hardships, in persecutions, in difficulties. For when I am weak, then I am strong."

Lest we should shudder at the thought of the trials that await us, 2 Timothy 3:12 reminds us that, *"Everyone who wants to live a godly life in Christ Jesus will be persecuted."* Jesus, often referred to as the Rose of Sharon, suffered tremendous pain and torture, even having a crown of thorns embedded on his head prior to being crucified, but it was worth it all when He rose triumphantly 3 days later. We too are promised a great reward but we have to endure the thorns first. Roses please.

104

On Target

Recently my husband and I were watching the Darts European Championships.[45] We were overawed at the skill of each of the competitors and just watching the competition caused us to reminisce about when we used to play the game many years ago. But what we used to do was nothing in comparison to what we witnessed. It was evident that these guys spent many years practising and consequently each game was simply incredible.

Players made it seem so easy but no matter how skillful each one was, at the end of each game only one person could emerge as the winner. Each man often hit his targets effortlessly, but occasionally he missed, especially at the very end and as a result it cost him the game. One of the most memorable matches was the final in which the defending champion was down 7-10. With one more game to win the challenger looked likely to cause an upset, but he faltered at a crucial time and the champion was able to claw his way back winning 11-10 to snatch victory from the jaws of defeat. Of course there was pandemonium in the arena. In like manner we have a target, set by Jesus Christ, which we need to work towards achieving. It is He who provides us with the standard to be followed.

We need to be careful however, in case we too falter at a crucial time.

Listen to what 2 Peter 1:5-11 says,

> [5]"*Make every effort to add to your faith goodness; and to goodness, [6]knowledge; and to knowledge, self-control; and to self-control, perseverance; and to perseverance, [7]godliness; and to*

---

[45] *Darts European Championships 2015*

godliness, mutual affection; and to mutual affection, love. ⁸For if you possess these qualities in increasing measure, they will keep you from being ineffective and unproductive in your knowledge of our Lord Jesus Christ. ⁹But whoever does not have them is nearsighted and blind, forgetting that they have been cleansed from their past sins. ¹⁰Therefore, my brothers and sisters, make every effort to confirm your calling and election. For if you do these things, ¹¹you will never stumble, and you will receive a rich welcome into the eternal kingdom of our Lord and Savior Jesus Christ."

We have to make sure that we walk circumspectly at all times and that our behaviour is consistent with Jesus' standards. One moment of indiscretion, lack of self-control or thoughtlessness could cost us. Should we step out of line at the wrong time we could be in danger of losing the prize, to which the apostle Paul alludes in Philippians 3:12-14,

¹²"Not that I have already obtained all this, or have already arrived at my goal, but I press on to take hold of that for which Christ Jesus took hold of me. ¹³Brothers and sisters, I do not consider myself yet to have taken hold of it. But one thing I do: Forgetting what is behind and straining toward what is ahead, ¹⁴I press on toward the goal to win the prize for which God has called me heavenward in Christ Jesus."

To do this, we need to stay on target.

105

What About The Fruit?

Mangoes, apples, oranges, bananas, melon, kiwi, strawberries, blueberries! There is no doubt that eating fruit is important to our overall health and wellbeing but when it comes to choosing between them and ice-cream or some other delectable pastry for dessert, many people usually choose the latter instead, despite them being more unhealthy. For a long time fruit was included mainly on dessert menus, but recent research has revealed that it is better to eat it before your meal, on an empty stomach, rather than after as has been the common practice. Incorporating fruit into one's diet, the proper way, causes the digestive system to benefit more through vitamin intake and improved digestion.

Consequently, your health and wellbeing are enhanced, you are able to avoid most digestive problems, you feel energized, weight loss is promoted and you are left looking and feeling fantastic because the body is fully absorbing all the vitamins, fibre and healthy carbohydrates which it needs to function. Interestingly, although the nutrients contained in fruit can help to guard against disease and lower rates of heart disease, stroke and high blood pressure, many people still opt out of choosing to eat it. Still, eating fruit carelessly, without any nutritional knowledge, could result in more problems to our health than benefits.[46]

The Bible speaks about fruit too - the fruit of the spirit.

> *"But the fruit of the Spirit is love, joy, peace, patience, kindness, goodness, faithfulness, gentleness and self-control. Against such*

---

[46] *Wikipedia Internet Reference* accessed 3rd November 2015

things there is no law. Those who belong to Christ Jesus have crucified the flesh with its passions and desires. Since we live by the Spirit, let us keep in step with the Spirit" (Galatians 5: 22) - and we are encouraged to incorporate it into our lives.

Just as there are benefits to be derived from eating natural fruit and following nutritional guidelines while doing so, eating haphazardly and without proper guidance - improper handling, storage, selection and/or preparation - can be detrimental to one's health. In like manner indiscriminate reading of the word, failing to seek proper guidance on it, interpreting it incorrectly and/or failing to follow what it says can affect one's spiritual health and cause long term damage.

We need to be disciplined and make a concerted effort though for as the apostle Paul warns us in Romans 7:15 and 18-19,

> [15]*"I do not understand what I do. For what I want to do I do not do, but what I hate I do.* [18]*...For I have the desire to do what is good, but I cannot carry it out.* [19]*For I do not do the good I want to do, but the evil I do not want to do - this I keep on doing."*

But the apostle offers us hope in verse 25 when he says, *"Thanks be to God, who delivers me through Jesus Christ our Lord!"*

So what about the fruit?

106

Of Recipes and Consistencies

As I have said on numerous occasions, though I like to eat, I am not a big fan of the kitchen. There is a saying, "The berry doesn't fall far from the tree, (unless of course it falls off a cliff)." When it comes to cooking though, I'll be the first to admit that I think I am the berry who fell off the cliff. Without a doubt I admire my late mother and aunt who were excellent cooks. I used to delight in saying, "I'm going home to eat my mother's food!" What struck me most about the two of them was the fact that they both seemed to have recipes stored in the forefront of their brain for easy retrieval and they always seemed to know how much of every ingredient was needed. Very much unlike me!

Banana bread has long been a favourite of mine and a few years ago I decided that instead of buying it when I wanted it I would start to make it. The first time I tried it though, it just didn't turn out quite like I had hoped. Though my husband and I ate it, we both agreed there was something about the consistency that was not right. I definitely couldn't share any of it with anyone. However, after finding the recipe in a cook book given to me by a friend and getting some tips from a few aficionados of the art I attempted the feat again and this time the outcome was so much better. I kept working at it until I had improved to the point that I was confident about sharing it with friends. And they were impressed! At least they said so. Imagine if I had ignored the recipe and the advice and had chosen to stick slavishly to what I had done the first time around! There would have been no improvements and I would not be sharing the delicacy.

In like manner in order for us to improve as individuals we need to follow the advice of James 1: 22-25,

22"Do not merely listen to the word, and so deceive yourselves. Do what it says. 23Anyone who listens to the word but does not do what it says is like someone who looks at his face in a mirror and, 24after looking at himself, goes away and immediately forgets what he looks like. 25But whoever looks intently into the perfect law that gives freedom, and continues in it – not forgetting what they have heard, but doing it – they will be blessed in what they do."

We need to keep working at making ourselves better and as we do we will have fewer flaws and become more consistent. 2 Chronicles 15:7 urges us, *"Be strong and do not give up, for your work will be rewarded."* God provides a flawless recipe, which, once followed, does not require any modification. If we adhere to His directions we will become a product of which He will be justly proud and He will reward us personally. Oh how tasty that will be!

107

By Whose Authority?

Power is an awesome thing. When used properly it can produce admirable results but if abused the effects can be devastating. When my father died some years ago he held the title of Justice of the Peace (JP). This enabled him to witness and certify copies of original documents and also gave him power to "keep the peace." I often smiled secretly as I listened to him threaten young offenders by telling them that he had the power to arrest them. I used to think then (and still do), "Which young man would allow a man of 78 years to arrest them?" But my dad was proud of his designation and knew that he would have the law to defend him should he require their backing.

At the end of my wedding ceremony the pastor presiding over the proceedings announced, "*By the power (in)vested in me I now pronounce you man and wife.*" This power was conferred on him by the government of that territory. Some pastors will argue even further that this authority comes first and foremost from Almighty God and based on that many refuse to perform same-sex marriages which, in their view, are contrary to God's law. Once, when being questioned by the Pharisees, Jesus replied, "*Haven't you read, that at the beginning the Creator 'made them male and female,' and 'For this reason a man will leave his father and mother and be united to his wife, and the two will become one flesh.*" (Matthew 19:5.)

In his letter to the Corinthian church the apostle Paul reiterates the point,

> "*Do you not know that wrongdoers will not inherit the kingdom of God? Do not be deceived: Neither the sexually immoral nor idolaters nor adulterers nor homosexuals, nor thieves nor the*

greedy nor drunkards nor slanderers nor swindlers will inherit the kingdom of God" (1 Corinthians 6:9).

It matters not what man thinks, does or legislates. It is what God declares that is important.

In 1 Samuel 17 when David went out to fight the giant Goliath, the diminutive shepherd boy declared to the Philistine,

> [45] *"You come against me with sword and spear and javelin, but I come against you in the name of the Lord Almighty, the God of the armies of Israel, whom you have defied.* [46]*This day the Lord will deliver you into my hands, and I'll strike you down and cut off your head. This very day I will give the carcasses of the Philistine army to the birds and the wild animals, and the whole world will know that there is a God in Israel.* [47]*All those gathered here will know that it is not by sword or spear that the Lord saves; for the battle is the Lord's, and He will give all of you into our hands."* 45:47

The rest is history: With no bodily armour and 5 pebbles and a sling, the little shepherd boy defeated the mighty giant. It is a great reminder that it is *'Not by might nor by power, but by [God's] Spirit'* (Zechariah 4:6) that we can overcome every obstacle facing us. It is not the local government or the seat of legislature that is the ultimate authority. Like David, we rely on the backing of Almighty God.

According to 2 Corinthians 10:4, *"The weapons we fight with are not the weapons of the world. On the contrary, they have divine power to demolish strongholds."* Because of this, *"No weapon formed against [the children of God] shall prosper,"* (Isaiah 54:17), and we will always emerge victorious when we decree, declare and go in the name of the Lord.

108

Crop Time

My parents were avid kitchen gardeners and apart from the regular cabbage, tomatoes, thyme, lettuce and parsley, they also planted pea trees, corn, yam, sweet potato and sugar cane. It was a lucrative business but it was hard. Though my contribution was limited, I recall that the tasks my brother, Joe, and I were asked to do such as "shelling" green peas and removing corn from the cob were finger-blistering activities. The most times we ventured onto the land was during the months of January and February when it was time to harvest the sugar cane.

My parents would co-opt my dad's sister and a couple of friends to cut the cane and my brother and I along with some other workers would walk behind them and create bands from the cut stalks, on which we would place the pieces of cane. These were then tied into bundles which were placed on a truck destined for the factory to be manufactured primarily into sugar. The best thing I liked about this time, however, was the opportunity afforded to suck the sugar from the cane! My father always tried to harvest his sugar crop early so as to avoid the dreaded fire bug which plagued some farmers at that time. Unlike the generous payments offered to farmers whose fields escaped this scourge, those with burnt canes suffered financially as they were not paid as much.

From a spiritual standpoint the fields of people are ready for harvesting. There are persons around us who are in danger of being burnt by hell fire if they are not rescued now. We, who are called by God, must make every effort to harvest them for the kingdom of God so that they can avoid a fiery end. The challenge, however, is in getting active workers on board. In Matthew 9:37-38 Jesus tells his disciples, [37]*"The harvest is plentiful but the workers are few. *[38]*Ask the Lord of the harvest, therefore, to send out workers into his harvest field."* There is also a reward promised for those involved in the harvesting according to John 4:36, *"Even now the one who reaps draws a wage and harvests a crop for eternal life, so that the sower and the reaper may be glad together,"* and, as stated in Daniel 12:3, *"Those who lead many to righteousness, will shine like the stars for ever and ever."*

It is Crop Time! Will you help?

109

Pottery 101

In the parish of St Andrew on the island of Barbados, there is a district called Chalky Mount, which is renowned for its pottery. Tourists and locals alike often visit the area to watch skilled artisans as they transform shapeless mounds of clay into beautifully crafted pots and jars. It is a messy affair, which requires a lot of skill but the end result is well worth it. Sometimes as the vessels are created there are some flaws, but the potter is never worried as he simply returns the piece to the wheel, adds some water to it and starts over. It is truly amazing.

According to Isaiah 64: 8 we too are like clay in the hands of God, the master potter, "*Yet you, Lord, are our Father. We are the clay, you are the potter; we are all the work of your hand.*" And as sovereign Lord, God reserves the right to shape us how He chooses. "*Can I not do with you, as this potter does?*" *declares the LORD. "Like clay in the hand of the potter, so are you in my hand. . ."* (Jeremiah 18:6)

He continues to work on each of us until we are made according to His specifications. Romans 9:21 declares, "*Does not the potter have the right to make out of the same lump of clay some pottery for special purposes and some for common use?*" When Adam and Eve were created they were made in the image of God, the creator, who expressed His pleasure at His masterpiece. "*God saw all that he had made, and it was very good*" (Genesis1:31).

We have all heard it said that God does not make junk. As Adam and Eve's descendants, we too have been well created in His own image. That is why the psalmist was able to declare, "*I praise you because I am fearfully and wonderfully made; your works are wonderful, I know that full well*" (Psalm 139:14).

Trials, however, are an integral part of the refining process, and according to Job 23:10 when God is through with us we will come forth as pure gold: *"But [God] knows the way that I take; when He has tested me, I will come forth as gold."* Though it may hurt at times, we should feel privileged that God continues to mould us and shape us on the wheel of His hands until we conform to His will and purpose for our lives, and like the songwriter we can say:

> *"Over and over, He moulds me and makes me,*
> *Into His likeness, He fashions the clay.*
> *A vessel of honour I am today*
> *All because Jesus didn't throw the clay away."*[47]

Enjoy/Endure your first lesson in Pottery 101. Keep it up and you could graduate magna cum laude!

---

[47] *He Didn't Throw the Clay Away*, Gene Reasoner, June 2000

110

WWW

If you are an internet user, you no doubt have encountered "www" whenever you have surfed the net. It was a while before I realised that it meant "world wide web." Not that knowing really mattered though. For some who are part of the 'modern' teaching fraternity, they may recognise "www" as part of the 'new lingo' associated with diagnostic marking, where it refers to "what went well." Whenever I have used abbreviations in writing these devotionals I have often delayed giving the meaning until right at the very end when I use it as a sort of punchline. I must admit I do derive a certain thrill when I know that my readers are assuming one thing only to discover I mean something completely different.

However, only recently a colleague and I were discussing how very frustrating it is to read articles or listen to speeches where the writer or speaker has used abbreviations only to leave their readers and listeners in total oblivion as they have absolutely no clue what the person means. So without further ado I will explain that the WWW in the title today stands for *'Watch While Walking.'* For many people walking is one of the preferred means of exercise. Some like to do it early in the morning, others later in the evening, with a few opting to go during the day, but whatever the choice there are certain tips usually offered for a safe journey. Walk facing on-coming traffic, avoid wearing dark clothing, wear reflectors and walk in single file are just a few pointers and depending on whether it is early morning or late in the evening, carry a flashlight. There is no guarantee that a mishap might not befall you but you do increase the probability of a safe walk if you follow these simple steps. Just as important is knowing where you intend to go.

The Bible also gives us some pointers about walking - walking with God that is. Jeremiah 6:16 states, *"This is what the LORD says: "Stand at the crossroads and look; ask for the ancient paths, ask where the good way is, and walk in it, and you will find rest for your souls."* Proverbs 4:14 also advises, *"Do not set foot on the path of the wicked or walk in the way of evildoers."* The reason for this is explained clearly in 1 Corinthians 15:33, *"Do not be misled: "Bad company corrupts good character."* You may ask, 'How can I win them over if I avoid them?' Well, you can let your actions do the talking. After all they do say that "Actions speak louder than words."

Matthew 5: 16 posits, *"Let your light shine before others, that they may see your good deeds and glorify your Father in heaven."* In order to accomplish this we must follow the command of Isaiah 2:5 and, *"Walk in the light of the LORD."* How is this done? The answer is explicit in Deuteronomy 10: 12,

> *"What does the LORD your God ask of you but to fear the LORD your God, to walk in obedience to him, to love him, to serve the LORD your God with all your heart and with all your soul."*

The Bible is replete with commands set out for us by God and it is important that we familiarize ourselves with them and make every effort to follow them accordingly. The psalmist David opines in Psalm 119:105 that, *"[God's] word is a lamp for [our] feet, a light on [our] path."* It is also important to teach God's ways to our children or those entrusted into our care, *"Impress them on your children. Talk about them when you sit at home and when you walk along the road, when you lie down and when you get up."* (Deuteronomy 6:7).

As free moral agents, however, God has given us the power to choose but whatever choice we make there are definite consequences.

Proverbs 28:18 makes it clear that, *"Those whose walk is blameless are kept safe, but those whose ways are perverse will fall into the pit."* It is true that sometimes we may deviate from the chosen pathway or stumble at times, but when this happens we should allow ourselves to be guided by Isaiah 30:21 which tells us that, *"Whether you turn to the right or to the left, your ears will hear a voice behind you, saying, "This is the way; walk in it."* And then. . . Just do it! Like natural muscles, which are developed as a result of engaging in habitual walking, when we continually read God's word and follow His precepts we begin to grow and mature spiritually to the point where we are like reflectors of who God is.

As we allow God's light to guide us and we guard our footsteps we are in fact becoming more formidable opponents against our common enemy, the devil. So it is important to Watch While Walking because, *"No good thing does [God] withhold from those whose walk is blameless"* (Psalm 84:11).

111

Simply The Best!

Only the best is good enough! Give of your best! Give it your best shot! Nothing but the best! These are just a few of the sayings that you often hear people use in order to encourage or compliment others. I don't know where the following originated but I was so impressed with it while growing up that I chose to use it some years ago as a clincher to an acceptance speech, after receiving an award for excellence in teaching:

> *Good, better, best*
> *Never let it rest*
> *'Til you make your good better*
> *And your better best!* [48]

It seems such an impressive jingle that it was the part included in the television clip later shown to local viewers. In a nutshell it says that people who have a real passion for excellence never rest on their laurels. As for mediocrity that does not feature at all as they are always yearning for something more, as "good" is just not good enough. It must be the best. We all want the "best" house, the "best" car, the "best" clothes, the "best" food, the "best" children etc. and we will spare no effort or expense to achieve these goals but when it comes to giving our "best" to God, who so lovingly gave these things to us in the first place, we fall woefully short.

We need to learn to put Him first in everything and as we do we will be richly rewarded. Matthew 6: 31 and 33, tell us, [31]*"So do not worry,*

---

[48] *Good Better, Best* St Jerome *Internet Reference* accessed 15th November 2015

saying, 'What shall we eat?' or 'What shall we drink?' or 'What shall we wear? . . . [33]*But seek first His kingdom and His righteousness, and all these things will be given to you as well."* But what does it mean to give your "best" to God? Simply put your "Best" is . . .

Behaviour that
Exudes excellence with
Superiority of success as
The Target

It is Behaviour that demonstrates outstanding Effort in giving of our Substance, Time and Talents, which all come from God and which should be offered to Him in gratitude for bestowing them so freely upon us.

Isaiah 48: 17 tells us that the know-how on being the best comes from God himself, "*This is what the LORD says-- your Redeemer, the Holy One of Israel: "I am the LORD your God, who teaches you what is best for you, who directs you in the way you should go.*"

Here are some questions which will help to determine whether we are on the right track with our current efforts:

- Do I have a talent that I don't use?
- Do I sometimes avoid church because I don't feel like going?
- Do I cite being too busy as a reason for not going to church or engaging in kingdom-building activities?
- Do I grumble sometimes when I am asked to do something which will help to build God's kingdom?
- Do I avoid volunteering when something has to be done to further the work of God?
- Do I read the word of God not as much as I should?
- Do I need to spend more time in prayer?
- Can I do more to witness to others?
- Can I give more to help others in need?

If the answer to any of these questions is "Yes" then we are NOT giving of our best to God and we are failing in our duty to Him. In giving of our "best" to God, we need to ensure that we demonstrate sustained brilliance as we aim to consistently go beyond the call of duty for Him. We were created to worship God and we can do this by giving of ourselves to Him totally and doing so as the songwriter says, "withholding nothing."

According to Philippians 1:9-10 it is important, [9]*"That your love may abound more and more in knowledge and depth of insight, [10]so that you may be able to discern what is best and may be pure and blameless for the day of Christ."*

The reward that awaits us is well worth the effort, time, talent and money that it will take. *"Let us not grow weary in well doing, for in due time we will reap a harvest of blessing if we don't give up."* (Galatians 6:9, Berean Study Bible.) *"I press on toward the goal to win the prize for which God has called me heavenward in Christ Jesus"* (Philippians 3:14).

Therefore let us be simply the best!

112

Mountain or Mole Hill?

Watching wrestling used to be one of my past-times in earlier days, until I saw a documentary which suggested that some of the matches had been fixed. They really had me fooled! Recently as I was flicking through the TV channels, I returned very briefly to my old habit.

A wrestling match was just about to begin. Prior to the match, one of the wrestlers was being interviewed. He was asked the question about whether his size might be a possible disadvantage against his much bigger opponent. His response: It's not the size of the dog in the fight; it's the size of the fight in the dog. Despite his puny frame he was not allowing himself to be intimidated by his opponent's size. Instead he believed that he had enough of a fighting spirit to secure victory and guess what? He won even though there were times when he looked like he might be defeated. In a mark of truly great sportsmanship the much larger wrestler, the vanquished, extended his hand to shake that of the conqueror's and then he raised it in the air as a form of acknowledgement.

Many a time I have heard persons say, "You're making a mountain out of a mole hill." From their viewpoint it seems that you are making more out of a situation than you need to while your perception of the matter may be completely different.

Mole hills can be crushed a lot more easily than a mountain can, but in Matthew 17:20 Jesus advocates, *"If you have faith as small as a mustard seed, you can say to this mountain, 'Move from here to there,' and it will move. Nothing will be impossible for you."* The devil will set up roadblocks but we are reminded in Isaiah 54:17 that, *"No weapon forged against you will prevail."* We have the power to remove obstacles put in our pathway by the devil and 1 John 4:4 tells us, "*You, dear children, are from God and have overcome them, because the one who is in you is greater than the one who is in the world.*"

To be an overcomer we need to pray in the name of Jesus which exudes power and deliverance and as we do we need to render every idea, every plan and every plot which the enemy will seek to establish against us, impotent. The key is to nip each mole hill in the bud before it blossoms into a towering mountain. And we have the weaponry to do so effectively according to 2 Corinthians 10:4, "*The weapons we fight with are not the weapons of the world. On the contrary, they have divine power to demolish strongholds.*" When we arm ourselves correctly and use our armour as intended we will be victorious. "*No, in all these things we are more than conquerors through him who loved us*" (Romans 8:37). We need not be afraid either because we have God's promise that He will be with us, "*Be strong and courageous. Do not be afraid or terrified . . ., for the LORD your God goes with you; he will never leave you nor forsake you*" (Deuteronomy 31:6). So remember it's not the size of the dog in the fight; it's the size of the fight in the dog.

It really only takes a teeny weeny bit of faith to change your circumstance. Look again! Is it really a mountain or is it in fact a mole hill?

113

Whatever

They say that language is constantly evolving. As time progresses meanings change and it is interesting how the definitions of words are becoming so different. Also interesting is how the word "evolve" has weaved its way into that expression. Evolution is an idea which contradicts the fact of creation.

I was amazed once when I searched the word "nice"[49] in a dictionary and found that in Old French it used to mean "simple," "silly" or foolish. I am sure that a growing number of young persons today only associate the word "gay" with "homosexual" and based on the reaction of many, some do not even know that it originally meant "merry and cheerful." That meaning has now been relegated to second spot according to Collins English Dictionary. There used to be a time when words like "wicked" and "bad" had evil connotations but these days depending on the context and one's intonation when using them they can be interpreted to mean quite the contrary.

The trend of assigning meanings so diametrically opposed to the original ones can be viewed as a subtle attempt to deceive, which brings us to the conclusion that the devil is the mastermind behind it all. There is no denying that he is a master counterfeiter and deceiver. John 10:10 describes him as a, *"Thief [who] comes only to steal and kill and destroy."* In recent years the real meaning of the word "whatever" has also been corrupted. When said with an attitude it is actually used as a form of rude dismissal. It is a far cry from the, "everything or anything that" definition. Unlike Satan, God, however, is immutable. He does not change. Malachi 3:6 tells us, *"I the Lord do not change."* His

---

[49] *Collins English Dictionary 2001*

word is unchangeable too. In Matthew 24:35, Jesus said, *"Heaven and earth will pass away, but my words will never pass away."*

He is also the epitome of truth and there is no corruption of meaning. *"I am the way and the truth and the life. No one comes to the Father except through me"* (John 14.6). God's meaning in John 14:13, is unequivocal, *"And I will do whatever you ask in my name, so that the Father may be glorified in the Son."* There should therefore be no hesitation in believing God when He says in Isaiah 1:18, *"Come now, let us settle the matter,"* says the LORD. *"Though your sins are like scarlet, they shall be as white as snow; though they are red as crimson, they shall be like wool."*

In conclusion, we are advised by the apostle Paul in Philippians 4:8, *"Finally, brothers and sisters, whatever is true, whatever is noble, whatever is right, whatever is pure, whatever is lovely, whatever is admirable – if anything is excellent or praiseworthy – think about such things."* There is definitely no shift in meaning here, whatsoever.

114

Is Everything Secure?

Make sure the alarm is on! Are the doors locked? Don't leave the windows open! We are living in a time when security is foremost in people's minds. Thefts of and from cars, businesses and homes seem to be an everyday occurrence and owners are doing everything in their power to secure their properties. It never ceased to amaze me how my late mother would lock the doors to her home but would leave her windows open whenever she was leaving. Her response to our caution against this practice was that people would definitely know she wasn't home if the house was all battened down! We always thought that she was taking chances but fortunately she was never a victim of a home invasion.

Unlike my mum though, some years ago my husband and I did suffer a break-in at our home despite being very cautious about closing and locking all windows and doors. As a matter of fact our neighbours on either side of us suffered the same fate that day. While one neighbour's door had been kicked in, the robber(s) used our own metal pole which we used as a door prop, to break our window. Through that hole a hand was inserted to push up the clip on the window and then turn the latch on the back door, through which easier access and eventual exit were made.

In an effort to make our property more secure we not only changed the lock systems on all doors, but my husband also installed an alarm system as well as a camera system. Our hurricane shutters also double as a deterrent. This is the route that many have taken in recent times but there are still stories of thieves circumventing even these systems. Isn't it ironic how we will go to extremes to protect our physical possessions which are only temporary and are guaranteed to fade away, but when it comes to our soul we are so carefree? Matthew 6:19-20 warns us,

> [19]"*Do not store up for yourselves treasures on earth, where moths and vermin destroy, and where thieves break in and steal.* [20]*But store up for yourselves treasures in heaven, where moths and vermin do not destroy, and where thieves do not break in and steal.*"

The warning is reiterated in Mark 8:36, "*For what shall it profit a man, if he shall gain the whole world, and lose his own soul?*"

Every bit of evil that we face is part of the devil's strategic plan to steal the souls of men, women and children. It is an integral part of the epic battle that has been ongoing between him and God since creation and is not simply a case of misfortune, envy, bad luck, karma, lawlessness or even the desire to take possession of property. Let there be no doubt about this for according to Jesus in John 10:10: Satan, described as a thief, has a plan, "The *thief cometh not, but for to steal, and to kill, and to destroy.*" Jesus on the other hand has, "*Come that [we] might have life, and that [we] might have it more abundantly.*" Sadly, some people put off making a decision for Christ under the misguided notion that they have time. 1 Thessalonians 5:2 tells us that Jesus' return will be unexpected as well, "*For you know quite well that the day of the Lord's return will come unexpectedly, like a thief in the night.*" For this reason it is imperative that persons commit their lives to Christ today as time, promised to no man, is slowly but surely running out. 2 Corinthians 6:2 is clear, "*Behold, now is the accepted time; behold, now is the day of salvation.*" For those of us who have already made that decision let us not become complacent. Let us follow the advice of 2 Peter 1:10 and, "*Make every effort to make [our] calling and election sure.*"

Now is the time to do a final check. Is everything secure?

115

In The Tunnel

While studying and vacationing in England, I often bought a day pass which enabled me to travel for the day on buses and trains in the different boroughs along sections of the route up to and including my final destination. Occasionally while travelling by train it would pass through a tunnel. For a brief moment outside became engulfed in darkness.

The first time I experienced it, the sudden change from light to dark was a bit scary but just as quickly as it came it disappeared. I soon realized that it didn't matter how long the tunnel was eventually light appeared at the end of it. However, until you reached close to the point when you could glimpse that flicker of light you were not sure where it was.

A friend of mine shared the following on my Facebook page: "When a train goes through a tunnel and it gets dark, you don't throw away the ticket and jump off. You sit still and trust the engineer." [50] I thought this was so thought-provoking. Imagine discarding your ticket and trying to get off just because you couldn't see where you were. You could miss arriving at your destination which could actually be just next to the exit of the tunnel. Instead we are called to place our faith in the one guiding the train.

I don't know whether it is a fact or not but I have often heard people say that the darkest part of the night is the time just before the dawn. When you are down in the doldrums of despair remember there is light at the end of your tunnel. Psalm 112:4 states, "*Even in darkness*

---

[50] *Facebook Reference* accessed 21ˢᵗ November 2015

light dawns for the upright, for those who are gracious and compassionate and righteous." Again in Psalm 30:5 the psalmist David says. *"For His anger lasts only a moment, but His favor lasts a lifetime; weeping may stay for the night, but rejoicing comes in the morning."*

You may be in the tunnel now but trust God regardless to how dark it is, because He is there with you and with Him as your driver you will surely come out in a much brighter place.

116

Fancy A Game Of Scrabble[51]?

When I first migrated to the Cayman Islands, my then room-mate and dear friend, Sandra, and I spent hours on end playing the popular word game Scrabble. I am forced to admit, albeit reluctantly, that she holds the record for the most wins.

It's amazing how as letters are added to existing words on the board the pronunciations of the newly formed words are changed and they assume different meanings. I recall, once, when Sandra added "re" to the word "al" and my first reaction was, "ree-al", what word is that? Of course, as she pointed out, it was the word "real!" We both laughed at my serious faux pas. It just goes to show how words can be so intriguing. Did you know that: "stressed" is "desserts" spelled backwards, out of "dedicated" we can get "dead" and the word "disappointed" contains the word "appointed"? The latter word comes from "appoint" which means "to assign officially to a job or a position or to fix or assign."

As children of God we have been positioned for greatness. We are indeed more than conquerors. 1 Peter 2:9 confirms this, *"But you are a chosen people, a royal priesthood, a holy nation, God's special possession, that you may declare the praises of him who called you out of darkness into his wonderful light."* However as human beings we often become disappointed when we think that decisions have not gone in our favour, but we ought to be reminded that each disappointment is part of God's assigned plan. He knows the end from the beginning and while it may be difficult to fathom at times, we are reminded in Isaiah 55:8, *"For my thoughts are not your thoughts, neither are your ways*

---

[51] *SCRABBLE® Wikipedia Reference* accessed 22nd November 2015

my ways," declares the LORD." God has great things in store for us and each perceived denial or delay is part of His master plan to give us something greater. Jeremiah 29:11 is clear *"For I know the plans I have for you," declares the LORD, "plans to prosper you and not to harm you, plans to give you hope and a future."*

So rather than being disappointed at the turn of events, now is the time to view each disappointment as an appointment from God. Man may disappoint but God appoints! Be encouraged with the words of Psalm 73:

1. *Surely God is good to Israel, to those who are pure in heart.*

2. *But as for me, my feet had almost slipped; I had nearly lost my foothold.*

3. *For I envied the arrogant when I saw the prosperity of the wicked.*

4. *They have no struggles; their bodies are healthy and strong.*

5. *They are free from common human burdens; they are not plagued by human ills.*

6. *Therefore pride is their necklace; they clothe themselves with violence.*

7. *From their callous hearts comes iniquity; their evil imaginations have no limits.*

8. *They scoff, and speak with malice; with arrogance they threaten oppression.*

9. *Their mouths lay claim to heaven, and their tongues take possession of the earth.*

10. *Therefore their people turn to them and drink up waters in abundance.*

11. *They say, "How would God know? Does the Most High know anything?"*

12. *This is what the wicked are like — always free of care, they go on amassing wealth.*

13. *Surely in vain I have kept my heart pure and have washed my hands in innocence.*

14. *All day long I have been afflicted, and every morning brings new punishments.*

15. *If I had spoken out like that, I would have betrayed your children.*

16. *When I tried to understand all this, it troubled me deeply*

17. *'Till I entered the sanctuary of God; then I understood their final destiny.*

18. *Surely you place them on slippery ground; you cast them down to ruin.*

19. *How suddenly are they destroyed, completely swept away by terrors!*

20. *They are like a dream when one awakes; when you arise, Lord, you will despise them as fantasies.*

21. *When my heart was grieved and my spirit embittered.*

22. *I was senseless and ignorant; I was a brute beast before you.*

23. *Yet I am always with you; you hold me by my right hand.*

24. *You guide me with your counsel, and afterward you will take me into glory.*

25. *Whom have I in heaven but you? And earth has nothing I desire besides you.*

26. *My flesh and my heart may fail, but God is the strength of my heart and my portion forever.*

27. *Those who are far from you will perish; you destroy all who are unfaithful to you.*

28. *But as for me, it is good to be near God. I have made the Sovereign Lord my refuge; I will tell of all your deeds.*

117

BFF

There are some people who will tell you that they have very few friends and then they will proceed to relate experiences they have had which have caused them to eliminate many persons from their inner circle, choosing to surround themselves with one or two loyal persons who will stick by them through thick and thin. It reminds me of something one of my former schoolmates used to say, "A friend in need is a pest!"

In attempting to justify this claim he explained that he had experienced many instances when so called friends always only wanted something from you or wanted you to do something for them. Many of us however, are more familiar with the saying, "A friend in need is a friend indeed." Best friends truly fit this description and though we live miles apart, I have one such friend called Kim. It is said that birds of a feather flock together, but I can tell you people are still baffled when they realize we are such close friends considering that she is such the quiet type while I am very outspoken and a little loud at times. Unlike me she always seems to be smiling and she does not get flustered so easily.

So what drew us together? I have no idea. I do not even recall our first meeting, but over the years we have grown closer, sharing intimate secrets and she has been a tower of strength and support. What is remarkable is that she has never once expected anything in return. I can only describe her care, concern and kindness as being overwhelmingly genuine and her presence in my life as a blessing from God. When I think of her I am reminded of Proverbs 17:17, *"A friend loves at all times, and a brother is born for adversity."* My fondest memory of her goes back several years ago when, as members of a netball team, we travelled to St. Thomas U.S Virgin Islands to represent the University of the West Indies. On the day of our departure, I decided that I wanted to do one last bit of shopping. Though there wasn't much time to spare before the flight, without a second thought Kim decided to accompany me. I can almost hear her now, "Jan, I am coming with you!"

When we returned all the other team members had already left and the two of us were left to find our way to the airport. On arrival we were told that we were too late and were denied boarding. We were then tasked with organizing our trip home via another airline. We had to take a longer route and the trip was not as comfortable. Fortunately there was a happy ending and incredibly in all of this not once did Kim complain or apportion any blame.

I have found her to be trustworthy and reliable so much so that power of attorney has been conferred on her to conduct business on my behalf. Lest you think that Kim is able to do all of this because she has so much free time at her disposal, she is not only an accountant by profession, but also the only daughter of ageing parents, whom she visits daily, the doting mother of a young boy, the loving aunt of two adorable nieces and a very active god-mother in the lives of her many god-children.

These are all sterling qualities for a friend to have, but as you can well imagine naturally there are times when she cannot fulfill an obligation immediately even though she may want to and will try to make every effort to. This may lead to disappointment but this should not be surprising for after all she is just human! However, according to Proverbs 18:24, *"There is a friend who sticks closer than a brother."* It is the God of the universe who offers us an even greater friendship. Kim and I have never had to risk our lives for each other but there is one person who loves each of us so much more that he laid down his life for us.

John 15:13-15 is clear,

> *"[13]Greater love has no one than this: to lay down one's life for one's friends. [14]You are my friends if you do what I command. [15]I no longer call you servants, because a servant does not know his*

master's business. Instead, I have called you friends, for everything that I learned from my Father I have made known to you."

If we our willing to turn our backs on what the world has to offer and place our unwavering trust in God we too can become His friend. James 2:23 tells us that, *"Abraham believed God, and it was credited to him as righteousness, and he was called God's friend,"* while in James 4:4 we are cautioned with the words, *"Don't you know that friendship with the world means enmity against God? Therefore, anyone who chooses to be a friend of the world becomes an enemy of God."*

If we allow him to, God can be our Best Friend Forever - and that's the Best Fundamental Fact!

118

The Boxer's Corner

Have you ever watched a boxing match? A constant feature is that after each 3-minute round boxers automatically go over to their corner where they sit and as they refresh themselves they listen attentively to the advice being given by their trainer. Once the contest has restarted it is ill-advisable to look towards the corner because an opponent will take advantage of any unguarded moment to knock you out.

The moment a fighter steps back into the ring it is up to him to put into practice what he has been taught and told. Occasionally he may be knocked down, but this does not have to be the end of the fight as he has until the count of ten to regain his footing and continue. That is of course unless the referee deems that it is safer for him not to do so. In that case he will stop the fight and the opponent will be awarded the fight by virtue of a TKO (Technical Knockout).

I have never really understood the logic of going into a ring and being beaten up, but I guess it is sport for some and it's a way of making one's livelihood for others. I certainly marvel at some fighters who despite repeated knockdowns and bloodied faces will keep getting up time and time again to continue the combat. It is even more incredible when they get up after a knock down to go on to win the match. The Christian life is very much like a boxing match and a lot can be learned from the kind of tenacity demonstrated by boxers.

The devil is a relentless opponent, but God is our coach/trainer, well skilled in the techniques we need to defeat our foe. As we face life's trials God is there to offer help and support. We need to be careful that we are not caught off guard because Satan will attempt to knock us out. It is important that we seek refuge from our trainer's corner. It is there that we will get the encouragement, assistance and guidance. Psalm 46: 1 states, "*God is our refuge and strength, a very present help in the time of trouble.*" Again in Psalm 16:8, we are told by the psalmist David, "*I keep my eyes always on the Lord. With Him at my right hand, I will not be shaken.*" Though we may be knocked down in the fight we don't have to stay down but we must struggle to get up again. It is only if we stay in the fight that we can have a chance at winning. 1 Timothy 6:12 encourages us to "*Fight the good fight of the faith. Take hold of the eternal life to which you were called when you made your good confession in the presence of many witnesses.*"

This is reiterated in the words of an old hymn:

> *Fight the good fight, with all thy might;*
> *Christ is thy strength and Christ thy right.*
> *Lay hold on life and it shall be*
> *Thy joy and crown eternally*[52].

With God in our corner victory is assured.

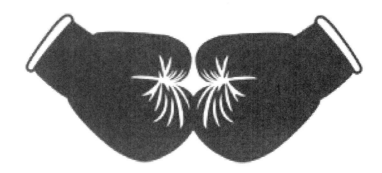

---

[52] *Fight The Good Fight,* John S. B. Monsell

119

Deal Or No Deal

Although watching TV is a form of relaxation for me, I must confess that it is one of my major weaknesses. Sometimes I actually spend hours on end watching the "idiot box" as some people call it and at times I have to make a concerted effort to pull myself away from it. While there are some shows I absolutely refuse to watch I do enjoy sports programmes and game shows, one of which is "Deal or No Deal."[53]

The first time I tuned into the show, the game had already started and I didn't have a clue what it was about, but after a few viewings the aim became clearer. The contest starts with 26 briefcases and revolves around the opening of a set of the numbered cases. While the values of each one, ranging from 1 cent to 1 million dollars, are known at the start of the game, their specific locations are not. The player begins by choosing a case, the value of which is not revealed until the conclusion of the game, to knock an amount of money off the board. There is also a very large board divided in two with the left side displaying the lower amounts while the right side shows the higher amounts. As the contestant chooses a case it is opened and the value revealed. It is then subtracted from the board.

By a process of elimination, the amount revealed cannot be inside the case the contestant initially claimed. Each player hopes to select as many cases with the lower amounts in order to enhance their prospects of winning the largest sum of money possible, preferably the million dollars. Throughout the game, after a predetermined number of cases have been opened, the banker offers the contestant an amount of money to quit the game, the offer based roughly on

---

[53] *Wikipedia Internet Reference* accessed 23rd November 2015

the amounts remaining in play and the contestant's demeanor. The bank tries to 'buy' the contestant's case for a lower price than what's inside the case. The game show host will ask "Deal or No Deal." Opting for "Deal" means the contestant will take the money offered and the game ends. If, however, "No deal" is selected then the game continues. It is amazing the number of times I have seen persons refusing what I consider to be very generous offers.

Often times I am sitting there shouting, "Deal, Deal" (as if they can hear me) and even though the contestant seems tempted to quit, sometimes they yield to the pressure from the audience or family members on set who are goading them on to continue and to my horror they say, "No Deal," and the game goes on. Once I watched a lady refuse a very generous offer from the banker only to continue and have all the large amounts eliminated.

The next time an offer was made it was much lower but left with few choices to get some real 'big' money she quickly accepted it. Isn't life somewhat like that game? Each day the devil sends temptations our way and he presents each one in a very attractive case. He lures us into thinking that the odds are greatly stacked in our favour because we cannot see what each "case" holds inside. If he didn't do it that way we would quickly ignore them. But don't be fooled! The devil has nothing good in store for any of us. After all he is the master of lies and his aim is to get us to yield. Hear what 1 Corinthians 10:13 tells us, "*No temptation has overtaken you except what is common to mankind. And God is faithful; He will not let you be tempted beyond what you can bear. But when you are tempted, He will also provide a way out so that you can endure it.*"

God will always provide a way of escape and He has promised us the best returns possible.

In John 14: 2 Jesus states,

> "*In my Father's house are many mansions: if it were not so, I would have told you. I go to prepare a place for you. And if I go and prepare a place for you, I will come again, and take you to be with me; that where I am, there you may be also.*"

God has promised us paradise which is far more precious than any other thing. Don't risk throwing it away by giving in to the devil's schemes. So next time you are tempted, don't yield and play Russian roulette with your soul but boldly rebuke the devil with an emphatic "No Deal" and make your deal with Jesus instead, who has promised in Revelation 22:12, *"And, behold, I come quickly; and my reward is with me, to give every man according as his work shall be."*

Deal or No Deal?

120

Roll Call

Educators everywhere will tell you that recording student attendance daily is very important and school authorities will justify their insistence on following this demand by warning each teacher that registers are legal documents and can be presented in court should there be probable cause to do so. For that reason they must be as accurate as possible, moreso too, in these days of graduation requirements, truancies and disappearances. Many business owners and leaders of other organisations also insist that workers sign in as part of attendance register procedures with some even requiring that employees indicate their time of arrival.

Providing a reasonable excuse which is supported by documented proof such as a doctor's certificate, in the case of illness, or a death certificate in the case of the loss of a loved one has also been added to the list of policies and procedures and depending on information received, absences may be classified as authorized or unauthorized and your take home pay and/or continued employment can be affected. Even in prison a daily roll call is in effect to ascertain that all prisoners are accounted for and alarms are raised when absences are not legitimate.

Some years ago I played the part of an old Christian lady in one of the scenes from the stirring and sobering production "Heaven's Gates, Hell's Flames". In the play I died of a heart attack and woke up at the entrance to the gates of Heaven. After admiring and commenting on the beautiful surroundings my eyes fell on an angel holding a huge book. My next line required me to ask, "Angel is my name written there?" The angel nodded and I was then met by King Jesus who ushered me into His presence. Oh what incredible joy! Conversely, however, there were scenes in which those who died faced a similar encounter but with far graver results. When asked "Is my name written there?" the angel, with a shake of the head, could only point towards "hell" and the screams of the actors and actresses were heart-wrenching as they were banished to their final destiny amidst the fiery flames.

Some may regard this as just a play but it is an enactment of Revelation 20:11-15 which suggests that there is coming a day when we will all stand before the judgement seat of Christ,

> [11]*Then I saw a great white throne and him who was seated on it. The earth and the heavens fled from his presence, and there was no place for them. [12]And I saw the dead, great and small, standing before the throne, and books were opened. Another book was opened, which is the book of life. The dead were judged according to what they had done as recorded in the books. [13]The sea gave up the dead that were in it, and death and Hades gave up the dead that were in them, and each person was judged according to what they had done. [14]Then death and Hades were thrown into the lake of fire. The lake of fire is the second death. [15]Anyone whose name was not found written in the book of life was thrown into the lake of fire.*

Whether people believe it or not, there will be a final roll call with an accompanying reward lasting for all eternity. There are many people who want to go to Heaven but according to Acts 4:12 the only sure way of being included on that register is by saying "Yes" to Jesus Christ and living a life that is pleasing to Him. *"Salvation is found in no one else, for there is no other name under heaven given to mankind by which we must be saved."* This is reiterated in Revelation 21: 27 which warns, *"Nothing impure will ever enter it, nor will anyone who does what is shameful or deceitful, but only those whose names are written in the Lamb's book of life."*

It is incumbent upon each one of us that we make sure that our names are recorded in the Lamb's Book of Life so that we can say with the songwriter, *"When the roll is called up yonder, I'll be there!*[54]*"*

---

[54] *When the Roll Is Called Up Yonder*, James Milton Black, 1893

ABOUT THE AUTHOR

Janet Dash-Harris was born in Coventry England where she lived with her parents Elton and Gwen and siblings, Cynthia, Gloria and Joseph. She attended Fredrick Bird's Infants and Junior Schools until her parents on the recommendation of the family doctor, decided to return to the warm climate of Barbados, the land of their birth.

In Barbados she received her primary education at St Andrew's Girls' School and Sharon Primary School before entering the Alleyne School in 1973.

After graduating in 1978 she continued A level studies at the Barbados Community College where she met and studied French and Spanish with her dear friend, Sandra Durant (now Yarde). On completion of her A levels she started work as a relief teacher in 1981 before going to work at the Ministry of Housing and Lands as a clerical officer. Following the birth of her son, in 1982 she entered the University of the West Indies to read for a degree in French and Spanish, but after 1 year withdrew to take up employment at Corcom West Indies Ltd, an Industrial firm, as Quality Assurance Clerk, later being promoted to Personnel Assistant.

After the closure of the company in 1984, she returned to the teaching fraternity and joined the staff of the Eagle Hall Primary School in 1985 for a brief stint before transferring to the West Terrace Primary School where she stayed for more than 12 years. A very competitive individual, she headed the school's Physical Education department and was responsible for leading it to its first ever National Primary Schools' Athletic Championships. She had the distinction of being the first female coach to lead a boys' football team to the finals of the Bico Primary School Football Tournament.

She entered Erdiston Teachers' College in 1986 and was elected as President of the Student Guild, graduating in 1988 as Student of the Year. It was while there that she met fellow student Janice Gibbs who extended an invitation for her to attend one of the special services being held at the Emmanuel Baptist Church. It was at that meeting that she first accepted Christ in 1987. She again returned to the University of the West Indies Cave Hill Campus in 1989 where she studied part-time graduating with honours in 1994 with a Bachelor of Arts in English and Linguistics with Education. In her first year she won the English award for the most outstanding student. In 1995 she travelled to Warwick University, England to study for a Master of Arts degree in English Language Teaching. After successful completion in 1996, she transferred to the Parkinson Memorial Secondary School where she taught English and Spanish and also successfully coached the U19 netball team to their first championships, defeating the then perennial champions.

After one year there, she migrated to the Cayman Islands in 1998 and continues to be a teacher of Spanish. The 2009 recipient of the Cayman Islands Chamber of Commerce Golden Apple Award for Excellence in Teaching at the Middle School Level, she has headed her school's Spanish Department since 2006 and is a former CXC Examiner in Spanish and Adjunct Lecturer in Spanish and English at the International College of the Cayman Islands (ICCI). She serves as an usher and Sunday School Teacher at the First Assembly of God Church, Grand Cayman and is a former member of the Church Board.

In 2001 she married Lincoln, whom she met while working at Corcom as the two vociferously supported rival teams. Known as a very outspoken person and a firm believer in equity and justice, the ardent sports enthusiast and former netballer is the mother of one son, Jamal and enjoys music, travelling and reading. This is her first published book.